The Way of
VINCENT
DE PAUL

Robert P. Maloney, C. M.

The Way of
VINCENT
DE PAUL

A Contemporary Spirituality
in the Service of the Poor

New City Press

Published in the United States by New City Press
86 Mayflower Avenue, New Rochelle, New York 10801
©1992 Robert P. Maloney, C. M.

Library of Congress Cataloging-in-Publication Data:

Maloney, Robert P.
    The way of Vincent de Paul : a contemporary spirituality in the
service of the poor / Robert P. Maloney.

    Includes bibliographical references.
    ISBN 1-56548-001-5 (pbk.) : $9.95
    1. Vincent de Paul, Saint, 1581-1660—Contributions in
spirituality.   2. Spirituality—Catholic Church—History—17th
century.   3. Catholic Church—Doctrines—History—17th century.
4. Vincentians—Spiritual life.   5. Daughters of Charity of St.
Vincent de Paul—Spiritual life.   6. Church work with the poor—
Catholic Church.   7. Vincentians—Rule.   8. Daughters of Charity of
Saint Vincent de Paul—Rule.   I. Title.
BX4700.V6M23   1992
255'.91—dc20   91-38205

1st printing: January 1992
3d printing: December 1992

Printed in the United States of America

CONTENTS

Preface 7

Acknowledgements 9

Introduction 11

Part I

Chapter I
The Christ of Vincent de Paul 19

Chapter II
Five Characteristic Virtues: Yesterday and Today 37

Chapter III
The Four Vincentian Vows: Yesterday and Today 70

Chapter IV
Community Living and the Community Plan 130

Part II

The Way of St. Vincent
A Rule for Servants of the Poor 145

PREFACE

The celebrated French historian, Henri Bremond, in his study of religious movements and personalities of seventeenth century France was captivated by the attractiveness and depth of spirituality that he encountered in the writings of Saint Vincent de Paul. He did not hesitate, however, to chide gently the Community of Saint Vincent for having too carefully guarded the writings of the Saint and for not having made them available to the public at large. He subsequently retracted his complaint when on the eve of the publication of his own magisterial work in the 1920's, he learned that the first volumes of the project of publishing the fourteen volumes of Saint Vincent's correspondence and conferences had begun to appear.

Father Bremond, were he writing today, might be justified in thinking and regretting that the English-speaking world was not yet sufficiently familiar with the writings of Saint Vincent. Language is a formidable barrier and the work of translation is demanding and slow. Recent years, however, have seen an acceleration in the pace of translating Saint Vincent's writings, as well as a growth in the number of studies of the many faceted mind and heart of Saint Vincent.

Among such studies must be placed the present volume—*The Way of Vincent de Paul*—which Father Robert Maloney offers to all who would like to become more acquainted with the spiritual vision of this man whose name immediately conjures up, not only the poor but the challenge of serving them. In a very painstaking and thorough manner Father Maloney presents, with ample references to sources, the outlines of Saint Vincent's "way." A feature of this work are the very practical deductions and consequences which Father Maloney draws out from the vows and virtues which Saint Vincent considered to be so important for a person called to serve Christ in the poor. This practical aspect of the book would, I feel, appeal greatly to Saint Vincent who considered prayer to be largely ineffective if it was not backed up by concrete resolutions bearing on one's daily life.

In welcoming this book—and in thanking Father Maloney—I feel confident that it will draw its readers closer to Saint Vincent whom Pope John Paul II has described as "a man of action and prayer, of administration and imagination, of leadership and humility, a man of yesterday and of today"

(Pope John Paul II to the Members of the General Assembly, 1986; cf. *Vincentiana* 1986, p. 416).

27 September 1991   Richard McCullen, C.M.
                                                       Superior General

ACKNOWLEDGEMENTS

Let me express my gratitude right from the start to the many people who helped me put this work together. Actually, most of the chapters originated in oral form in a series of conferences to the Daughters of Charity. Subsequently, using those materials, I published a series of articles in *Vincentiana,* whose immediate audience was the Vincentian community of priests and brothers. The reader will undoubtedly note remnants of both the original "oral tradition" and then the "written sources." After some hesitation, I decided not to obliterate those remnants, since often their concreteness, though revealing that they were originally directed to a particular group (male or female), gives life to what otherwise might remain merely theoretical. All of the chapters have been revised—some extensively, some less so—in preparing this book. I address it primarily to the extended Vincentian family, which includes the members of the Congregation of the Mission, the Daughters of Charity, a large number of other communities of sisters, and hundreds of thousands of other lay Vincentians throughout the world, but I hope that it will also be of service to others who seek to give their lives in the service of the poor.

I want to express my sincerest thanks to those who assisted in the nitty-gritty labor of putting the book in its final form: to Julie Keating, Barbara Spigel, and Llewellyn Sasyn, who did much of the typing in its early stages; to Fran Japertas, Colleen Kleintop, and Helen Neveroski, who typed the computerized version; to Jim Claffey and Pat Griffin, who lodged me and offered me generous computer services during the revision stage; and to my sister Marie, for proofreading the text. The simple truth is that without such help books do not get written.

May God instill in you . . . a deep love for Our Lord Jesus Christ, who is our father, our mother, and our all.

SV V, 534

INTRODUCTION

He just about transformed the face of the Church!

Henri de Maupas du Tour
Funeral Oration of St. Vincent[1]

A few years ago, as I was preparing for a talk on Vincentian spirituality, I went to a wonderful exhibit of Claude Monet's paintings. Three of them intrigued me especially. Each showed exactly the same location on the Seine—one at dawn, one at midday, one at dusk. Each had a beauty of its own. In the first, gauze-like rays of light filtered through the heavy morning mist that lay on the river. In the second, the face of the river was bathed in sunlight, and the bright green of the trees and the yellow and red of the flowers on the river banks sparkled with light. In the third, long shadows stretched out over the river and only a gentle purple glow lit the evening sky. They were very different views of the same reality, and through them Monet was illustrating an important lesson: we cannot exhaust a reality by fixing on it at a single moment or from a single point of view.

It is much the same with the gospels. When they look at the rich reality of Jesus, they can only attempt to express it in pieces and from varying points of view. The Jesus of Mark is very human in his ignorance; the Jesus of John shares the knowledge of God as he reads the future. In the gospels we see Jesus as Lord, but we also see him as suffering servant. We see him forcefully confronting the Pharisees. We see him meek as a lamb led to the slaughter. We find an ascending Christology and a descending Christology, and several in-between.

The saints are similar. It is not easy to capture their richness in a single word or a single phrase. A still photo of St. Vincent or St. Francis of Assisi would not tell the whole story. They did not live merely at a single moment in time, nor in a single place. Neither were they influenced merely by one

---

1. This quotation is cited by André Dodin, in *St. Vincent de Paul et la Charité* (Paris, 1960) 103: "Il a presque changé la face de l'Eglise."

11

person. Nor did they perform merely one work. The saints' vision of Jesus was rich, and like the many facets of a bright diamond, their lives sparkle before our eyes in varying ways.

That is, of course, why people argue over what the core of St. Vincent's spirituality is. In describing it, some focus on doing the will of God, others on following providence. Some see the core as his way of integrating prayer and action; others stress simplicity and humility. Some, perhaps most understandably, say that service of the poor is everything for St. Vincent and is the driving force behind whatever else he did, including his work in forming the clergy. All speak an element of the truth. Yet all somehow fall short. Each expresses an aspect of St. Vincent's spirituality, but each fails to do justice to the whole, to the context into which the various elements fit.

So too, what I have written below is a partial, inadequate effort, as I attempt to describe the spirituality of St. Vincent.

The Christ of St. Vincent has long fascinated me. "He described himself as the Evangelizer of the Poor," St. Vincent writes.[1] It is this Christ who lies at the heart of St. Vincent's spirituality.

But that is to run ahead of the story. First, a very brief word about St. Vincent; secondly, a word about spirituality in general; and then finally, a word about Vincentian spirituality.

1. A word about St. Vincent

This remarkable man, born at Pouy in southern France in 1581, had a rather self-seeking start in the priesthood. Under the influence of spiritual directors like St. Francis de Sales, Cardinal Bérulle, and André Duval, he underwent a striking conversion, in which he gave his life over to God in the service of the poor. He founded the Congregation of the Mission (1625), a community of priests and brothers whose end is "to preach the good news to the poor" and the Daughters of Charity (1633), at that time a new form of community in which the sisters lived "in the world" to serve the sick poor spiritually and corporally. He also established the Confraternities of Charity (lay organizations, both of men and women, founded in parishes also to assist the poor spiritually and corporally) and the Ladies of Charity; these groups continue to the present day in very large numbers. Eager for the reform of the clergy, he organized retreats for ordinands and founded seminaries

---

1. SV XI, 32. *SV* refers to the fourteen volume French edition of St. Vincent's works, edited by Pierre Coste (Paris: Gabalda, 1920-25). I have used Joseph Leonard's translations as a starting point, but have often modified these in light of the original text.

throughout France. He gathered together many of the clergy of his day each Tuesday, both in Paris and elsewhere, for conferences. Born a Gascon peasant, he became the counsellor of King Louis XIII, to whom he ministered on his deathbed, and of Queen Ann of Austria, and was the friend and confidant of saints like Francis de Sales, Jane Frances de Chantal, Alain de Solminihac and Louise de Marillac. When he died on September 27, 1660, all of Paris mourned him. He is known throughout the world today as the Patron of Charity. His spirituality lives on in hundreds of thousands of lay men and women, priests, sisters and brothers who follow in his footsteps.

2. A word about spirituality

A spirituality is an energizing vision, a driving force. It is, on the one hand, the specific way in which a person is rooted in God. It is, on the other hand, the specific way in which he or she relates to the created world. It is insight as the source of action. It is a vision that generates energy and channels it in a particular direction, thereby enabling a person to transcend himself or herself. For the Christian, it is a way of seeing Christ and being in him that directs the individual's energies in the service of the kingdom.

Contemporary writers emphasize the transcendent thrust of all spirituality, both Christian and non-Christian. Sandra Schneiders describes it as "the experience of consciously striving to integrate one's life in terms not of isolation and self-absorption but of self-transcendence toward the ultimate value one perceives."[1] The main characteristics of spirituality, largely agreed on by theologians today, are included within this definition: progressive, consciously pursued, personal integration through self-transcendence within and toward the horizon of ultimate concern, which in St. Vincent's case is Christ the Evangelizer of the Poor.

3. A word about Vincentian spirituality

Naturally, the spirit of the Vincentian family flows from the spirit of its founder. The Constitutions of the Congregation of the Mission give a schematic description of that spirit, which is at the same time a very good description of St. Vincent's spirituality, though, for the reasons mentioned above, necessarily an incomplete one.

---

1. Sandra Schneiders, "Spirituality in the Academy," *Theological Studies 50* (1989), 684; cf. also, by the same author, "Theology and Spirituality: Strangers, Rivals, or Partners?" *Horizons* 13 (1986), 266.

Here, let me offer a brief schema of that spirit based on articles 4-7 of the Vincentian Constitutions of 1984:

THE VINCENTIAN SPIRIT IS THE SPIRIT OF CHRIST AS SENT TO PREACH
THE GOOD NEWS TO THE POOR[1]
AS EVIDENCED IN THE GOSPEL SAYINGS EXPLAINED IN THE COMMON RULES[2]
CONCRETIZED PARTICULARLY THROUGH:
LOVE AND REVERENCE TOWARDS THE FATHER
COMPASSIONATE AND EFFECTIVE LOVE FOR THE POOR
DOCILITY TO DIVINE PROVIDENCE[3]
SIMPLICITY
HUMILITY
MEEKNESS
MORTIFICATION
ZEAL FOR SOULS[4]
"JESUS CHRIST IS THE RULE OF THE MISSION"[5]
AND THE CENTER OF ITS LIFE AND ACTIVITY[6]

There is room for much meditation here, even for an entire retreat. Notice that, when the Vincentian Constitutions present a vision of the Vincentian spirit, it is *unified* in one respect: it flows from a vision of Jesus Christ as the Evangelizer of the Poor. But it is *diversified* in another respect: the riches, the ramifications, of that vision are many.

It is evident that St. Vincent has made a clear choice. The vision he offers his followers is a vision of Christ not as teacher (as might be the vision of a Christian Brother), nor as healer (as might be the vision of a community dedicated to hospitals), but as the Evangelizer of the Poor. Vincentians are called to enter into the Lucan journey of the following of Christ in the very terms with which, in Luke's gospel (4:18), Jesus opens his public ministry: "The Spirit of the Lord is upon me; therefore, he has anointed me. He has sent me to bring glad tidings to the poor, to proclaim liberty to captives, recovery of sight to the blind and release to prisoners, to announce a year of favor from the Lord."

St. Vincent's spirituality flows from his contemplation of *this* Christ. It is

---

1. C 5.
2. C 4.
3. C 6
4. C 7.
5. SV, XII, 130.
6. C 5.

the spirit of the Evangelizer himself, alive and acting in St. Vincent's and our world. It expresses itself in love and reverence for the father, compassionate and efficacious love for the poor, in docility to providence, and in the five missionary virtues of simplicity, humility, meekness, mortification, and zeal.

Those who live in the Vincentian spirit are called to contemplate *this* Christ again and again. He is the rule of the Mission.

This Christ of Luke 4:18 stands at the center of the spirituality of the members of the Vincentian family, calling them to walk with him on his journey. Without him, the journey is aimless, empty. Of this Christ, St. Vincent might repeat to his followers the striking words of Deuteronomy: "Bind his name on your hands. Let it be a pendant before your eyes. Let it be written on the doorposts of your houses so that you may see it in your coming in and your going out" (cf. Dt 6:8-9).

This book will attempt to speak about various aspects of a Vincentian spirituality, which I describe below in graphic form:

CHRIST THE EVANGELIZER OF THE POOR

Gospels
Common Rules

Love and reference toward the Father	Simplicity
Compassionate & effective love for the poor	Humility
Docility to providence	Meekness
	Mortification
	Zeal for souls

PART I

I ask Our Lord to be himself your strength and your life, as he is for all those who are nourished by his love.

SV VIII, 15

Chapter I

THE CHRIST OF VINCENT DE PAUL

Let us walk with confidence on this royal road on which Jesus Christ will be our mentor and guide.

SV XI, 52

A strong current in recent theological literature stresses the importance of the saints as a theological source.[1] The saints, these writings emphasize, rescue theology from excessive abstraction. They root it in life and give it flesh. In doing so, they deepen and enrich it. In that sense, they are one of its most valuable fonts.

Other trends in contemporary theology reinforce this movement. We are more and more conscious today, first of all, of the inseparability of theology and spirituality, even though, since the fourteenth century (and all the more so since the time of the Reformation), each has tended to go its separate way. We profess today that healthy spirituality depends on valid theological underpinnings and that, conversely, healthy theology is continually revitalized by the insights of the spiritual masters. Secondly, we are increasingly aware that theology and praxis, or—to observe the order used by liberation theology—praxis and theology, necessarily influence one another. Thus, we find a renewed interest in the saints as known through critical biographies that employ scientific methodology; besides their value as hagiography, such works serve as sources for the contemporary "doing of theology."

The purpose of this chapter is to describe the christological vision of Vincent de Paul. The reader will soon note that the evidence, as I read it, shows that the Christ of St. Vincent has a decidedly Lucan character. But to avoid confusion, let me make three clarifications about this right from the start:

1. First, by no means do I contend that Vincent's view of Christ is *exclusively* Lucan. Like most saints, he drank from more than one source. One of his favorite texts, for example, is Matthew 25:31-46. In fact, he cites

---

1. For an ample bibliography, cf. William M. Thompson, *Fire and Light, The Saints and Theology* (New York: Paulist, 1987) 7.

19

Matthew's gospel considerably more frequently than Luke's and, as will be explained below, draws significant themes from both John (e.g., the stress on Jesus' communion with the Father and on practical love of the neighbor) and Matthew (e.g., Jesus' emphasis on truthfulness and gentleness).[1]

2. Nor is it my contention that Vincent's view of Christ is *explicitly* Lucan. No one would claim that Vincent de Paul was a systematic theologian. For him praxis was more important than theory. He had a distrust of intellectual curiosity[2] and encouraged action much more than scholarship.[3] He employs a christological framework which he learned from masters like de Bérulle,[4] Francis de Sales[5] and André Duval,[6] but it remains largely implicit. He does not speak or write about Christology as such. But he often speaks and writes of Christ; even more clearly, he develops a way of "living" Christ and teaches it to his followers. The vision he imparts is significantly different from that of his teachers.[7]

---

1. In the conferences to the missionaries, St. Vincent cites Matthew 199 times; Mark, 28; Luke, 84; John, 86; cf. A. Dodin, "La inspiración evangélica de la doctrina vicenciana," in *San Vicente de Paul, Pervivencia de un Fundador*. I Semana Vicenciana (Salamanca, 1972) 35.
2. *Common Rules of the Congregation of the Mission* XII, 8; henceforth, CR.
3. In a wonderful letter to François du Coudray, who was asking permission to remain in Rome to translate the Syriac Bible into Latin, he writes, with some considerable feeling: "Picture to yourself then, sir, that there are millions of souls with outstretched hands calling you saying: 'Ah, M. du Coudray, you who have been chosen from all eternity by the providence of God to be our second redeemer, have pity on us. We are wallowing in ignorance of the things necessary for our salvation and in the sins that we have never dared to confess, and for want of your help we will certainly be damned' " (SV I, 252).
4. Cf. Michel Dupuy, "Le Christ de Bérulle," *Vincentiana* 30 (1986), 240-52. Vincent was influenced by Bérulle particularly from 1609 to 1617. He learned from him especially a sense of the priestly ministry of Christ. Bérulle's is an abstract, descending Christology, with a heavy emphasis on the divine attributes of Christ. Heavily influenced by Scotism, Bérulle characterizes Jesus as destined from all eternity, whether the human race should fall or not, to be the "perfect adorer of the Father." He is totally ruled, possessed, penetrated by the Father. He is at once servant, priest, victim.
5. Cf. Helène Bordes, "Le Christ de François de Sales," *Vincentiana* 30 (1986), 253-279. From about 1618 until his death in 1622, Francis had a great influence on Vincent de Paul, who regarded him as a model of gentleness, joy, and affability. Much of Vincent's teaching on detachment and indifference relies heavily on Francis' doctrine. Vincent modifies Francis' teaching about the practice of the presence of God and develops it into the practice of doing the will of God in all things. For Francis, Christ is the "perfect image of the divinity." At the same time Christ lives the perfection of humanity in all the stages of his existence: his birth, his hidden life, his public life, his passion and death, his resurrection.
6. Antonino Orcajo, "San Vicente de Paul: fe y experiencia en una doctrina," in Antonino Orcajo and Miguel Pérez Flores, *San Vicente de Paul, II. Espiritualidad y selección de escritos* (Madrid: BAC, 1981) 63-65, 101-102. Duval, whom St. Vincent described (SV XI, 128) as "so wise and at the same time humble and simple that you could not ask for more," was also of the abstract school of Christology. He was St. Vincent's counsellor from around 1617 until his death in 1638, a period marked by some of the most important decisions relating to Vincent's foundations.
7. Cf. Luigi Mezzadri, "Jésus-Christ, figure du prêtre-missionaire dans l'oeuvre de Monsieur Vincent," *Vincentiana* 30 (1986), 327; also cf. A. Dodin, *op.cit.*, 36.

3. My objective in this chapter is to describe the Christ of Vincent, not to prove that this Christ is decidedly Lucan. But my reading of the evidence is that, while Vincent is influenced by many sources, Luke's gospel plays an especially important role.

Since much of St. Vincent's Christology is implicit, my aim in the pages that follow is to uncover, by making it explicit, the christological vision that grounds Vincent's thought and action and that lies at the heart of his spirituality.[1]

As mentioned in the introduction to this book, a specific spirituality is a governing vision. But more than a vision, it is a driving force, enabling a person to transcend himself or herself.[2] It is, on the one hand, the specific way in which a person is rooted in God. It is, on the other hand, the specific way in which he or she relates to the created world. It is insight as the source of action. It is a world-view that generates energy and channels it in a particular direction.

For Vincent de Paul, there is only one driving force: the person of Jesus Christ. "Jesus Christ is the Rule of the Mission,"[3] he tells the members of the Congregation of the Mission, the center of their life and activity. "Remember, Father," he writes to Monsieur Portail, one of the original members of the Congregation, "that we live in Jesus Christ by the death of Jesus Christ and that we ought to die in Jesus Christ by the life of Jesus Christ and that our life ought to be hidden in Jesus Christ and full of Jesus Christ and that in order to die like Jesus Christ it is necessary to live like Jesus Christ."[4]

Vincent warns his followers that they will find true freedom only when Christ takes hold of them. He writes to Antoine Durand, the newly appointed superior of the seminary at Agde: "It is therefore essential for you, Father, to empty yourself in order to put on Jesus Christ."[5]

---

1. For other attempts along these same lines, the reader might wish to consult the articles by Dodin and Mezzadri cited above; cf. also C. Riccardi, "Cristologia e cristocentrismo vincenziani," *Annali della Missione* 88 (1971), 51-76; I. Fernández-Mendoza, "La Cristología en la vida y pensamiento de San Vicente de Paul," *Anales* 93 (1985), 598-612.
2. For a comprehensive discussion of the meaning of spirituality and its relationship to theology, cf. Sandra Schneiders, "Theology and Spirituality: Strangers, Rivals, or Partners?" *Horizons* 13/2 (1986), 253-74.
3. SV XII, 130; cf. also XI, 53: "Let us walk with assurance on the royal road on which Jesus Christ will be our guide and leader."
4. SV I, 295.
5. SV XI, 343-44.

DISTINCTIVE CHARACTERISTICS OF THE CHRIST
OF VINCENT DE PAUL

Jesus' question to his disciples remains the fundamental christological question in every age. "And you?" he asks (Mt 16:15), "Who do you say that I am?"

The response of Vincent de Paul, framed in the conventional theological language of seventeenth-century France, is an existential one. It relates Jesus to his *mission*. In his writings and conferences, Vincent frequently uses the biblical titles "Christ," "Lord," "Son of God" to describe Jesus. In this, he reflects the accepted terminology of the day, almost always without analyzing it.[1] But a study of Vincent's works reveals that, moving beyond this terminology, his vision focuses on the *missionary* Christ.[2]

How, then, does he answer the perennial christological question: who do you say that I am? In response, let me outline several of the most important characteristics of the Christ of Vincent de Paul.

1. Christ is the Evangelizer of the Poor

Vincent de Paul returns to this theme again and again. In perhaps his most famous conference, on "The End of the Congregation" (December 6, 1658), he states: ". . . to make God known to the poor, to announce Jesus Christ to them, to tell them that the kingdom of heaven is at hand and that it is for the poor. O how great that is . . . so sublime is it to preach the gospel to the poor that it is above all the office of the Son of God."[3] In another conference, he says: "In his passion, he had scarcely the appearance of being human. In the eyes of the gentiles he passed for a fool. To the Jews he was a stumbling block. But with all that, he described himself as the Evangelizer of the Poor: 'To preach the good news to the poor he has sent me.' "[4]

Vincent makes a clear explicit choice.[5] The vision he offers is not one of

---

1. Nowhere, for example, do we find St. Vincent analyzing the origins of these titles (in Palestinian Judaism or in the Hellenistic world), their meaning, or their application to Jesus.
2. This approach is similar to that of much contemporary christological reflection. Cf. Elizabeth Johnson, *Consider Jesus. Waves of Renewal in Christology* (New York, 1990), especially 51-57.
3. SV XII, 80.
4. SV XI, 32. While a given reader may doubt that this text (calling Christ "the Evangelizer of the Poor"), attributed to St. Vincent by Abelly, his first biographer (1664), conveys the *ipsissima verba* of the saint, the idea itself, nonetheless, seems to me indisputable, given St. Vincent's repeated recourse to Luke 4:18.
5. Cf. also SV X, 123; XII, 262: "All aim at loving him, but they love him in different ways:

Christ as teacher,[1] nor as healer,[2] nor as "perfect adorer of the Father" (Bérulle's vision), nor as "perfect image of the divinity" (the vision of Francis de Sales), but as *The Evangelizer of the Poor*. Vincent's disciples are called to enter into the following of Christ in the very terms with which, in Luke's gospel, Jesus opens his public ministry: "The Spirit of the Lord is upon me; therefore, he has anointed me. He has sent me to bring glad tidings to the poor, to proclaim liberty to captives, recovery of sight to the blind and release to prisoners, to announce a year of favor from the Lord" (4:18).[3]

This is a distinctively Lucan theme. Luke deliberately transposes and edits the scene of Jesus' visit to the synagogue at Nazareth, so that it takes place at the beginning of the public ministry. The result is a new composition which Luke makes programmatic for the rest of his account of that ministry, with Jesus applying to himself the words of Isaiah 61:1-2. Luke reiterates this theme and further develops it in 7:21-22.[4] In Luke's perspective, a new age is dawning. Jesus announces the good news of the kingdom to all, but especially to the poor, the weak, the lowly, the outcasts of the world:

* happy are you poor (6:20)
* the poor have the good news preached to them (7:22)
* when you go to a banquet, invite the poor (14:13)
* go through the streets and bring here the poor (14:21)
* a beggar named Lazarus lay at the door . . . this poor man (16:20-22)
* sell all that you have, give it to the poor (18:22)
* Lord, I give half of my goods to the poor (19:8)
* this poor widow put in more than all the others (21:3)

Because of this emphasis, Luke's gospel is sometimes called the "Gospel of the Poor."

St. Vincent's spirituality flows from his contemplation of *this* Christ. The driving force that generates both the incredible activity and the gentle contemplation of this great saint is his vision of the Evangelizer of the Poor.[5] He encourages his followers to contemplate this Christ again and again. "O how

Carthusians by solitude; Capuchins by poverty; others, again, by singing his praises. But we, my brothers, are bound to show it by leading the people to love God and their neighbor."

1. Cf., for example, Lk 7:20; 9:38; 10:25; 11:45; 12:13; 18:18; 19:39; 20:21, 28, 39; 21:7. The title appears frequently in the New Testament.
2. This image of Jesus too was very important in the mind of the evangelists; cf., for example, Mk 1:29f.; Mt 8:1f.; 9:1f.; 9:18f.; Lk 7:1f.; 13:10f.; Jn 9:1f.
3. Scriptural citations are from the New American Bible translation. But scriptural texts within quotations from St. Vincent are translated directly from his French text.
4. J. Fitzmyer, *The Gospel According to Luke I-IX*. Anchor Bible (Garden City, NY, 1981) 248; cf. also 529, 532.
5. Mezzadri points out how forcefully St. Vincent's concrete vision of Christ as coming in the service of the poor influenced his view of the formation of the clergy; cf. *op. cit.*, 330-32.

happy will they be who can repeat at the hour of their death those beautiful words of Our Lord: 'He sent me to preach good news to the poor.' "[1]

2. Christ comes to liberate his people, to release them from the bondage of their corporal and spiritual wounds

Vincent's view of Jesus' evangelizing activity is a broad one.[2] This is clear in the mandates that he gives to the various groups he founded: the Congregation of the Mission, the Daughters of Charity, the Confraternities of Charity, and the Ladies of Charity.

Jesus comes ". . . to proclaim liberty to captives, recovery of sight to the blind and release to prisoners, to announce a year of favor from the Lord" (Lk 4:18). He comes to "save his people from their sins" (Mt 1:21; cf. Lk 1:77). Both these aspects of Christ's mission lie at the heart of St. Vincent's ministry.

The *mission* was the primary work of the company of priests and brothers Vincent founded. It aimed at conversion and culminated in the sacrament of penance, particularly in the general confession.[3] He presented this work to the members of his Congregation as the vocation of the Son of God.

Late in life St. Vincent recalled with warmth the event that inspired the founding of the Congregation of the Mission: "It was in the month of January 1617 that it happened. On the Feast of the Conversion of St. Paul, which falls on the 25th, this woman begged me to preach a sermon in the church at Folleville to exhort the inhabitants to make a general confession. I did so and pointed out to them the importance and usefulness of this practice. I then taught them how to make it well. God had such a regard for the confidence and good

---

1. SV XI, 135. Though he spoke at times in lyrical language about the service of the poor, St. Vincent had by no means a romantic view of this ministry. Cf. SV XI, 32: "I should not judge poor peasants, men or women, by their exterior, nor by their apparent mental capacities. All the more is this so as very frequently they scarcely seem to have the appearance or mental capacity of reasonable beings, so gross and earthy are they. But turn the medal and you will see by the light of faith that the Son of God, whose will it was to be poor, is represented to us by these creatures. . . ."

2. Cf. *Evangelii Nuntiandi*, 30-39; Congregazione per la Dottrina della Fede, *Istruzione su "Libertà cristiana e liberazione"* (March 22, 1986) 99. While Vincent was very aware of the need to meet the social problems of his day with structured, institutionalized solutions (e.g., through the societies he founded), he was, nonetheless, like most of his contemporaries, largely unaware of what today we might call "sinful social structures." For the most part, he accepted the existing political and social order as it was (as did St. Paul, for instance, in regard to slavery). Still, within that context, he saw the need for political action as he addressed the needs of the poor and used his influence in court and on the Council of Conscience to that end. Cf. Luigi Mezzadri, *San Vincenzo de Paul* (Edizioni Paoline: Milan, 1986) 69-79; 83-86.

3. SV I, 58-59; 562-63.

faith of this woman . . . that he blessed my discourse, and all those good people were so touched by God that all came to make a general confession. . . . That was the first sermon of the Congregation of the Mission. . . ."[1]

In his conferences and letters, he envisions a Christ who reaches out to sinners, with a confident hope in their forgiveness and amendment. "O Savior! How happy were those who had the good fortune to approach you! What a countenance! What meekness, what openness of manner you showed in order to attract them! With what confidence you inspired people to approach you! O, what signs of love!"[2] He frequently focuses on the heart of Jesus: "Let us look at the Son of God. O, what a loving heart! What a flame of love."[3] It is because of his tender love that the Word becomes flesh: "Ah, how tender the Son of God was! . . . This tender love was the cause of his coming down from heaven. He saw men deprived of his glory. He was touched by their misfortunes."[4]

Jesus' tender love for sinners is another distinctively Lucan theme:[5]

* the sinful woman (7:36-50)
* the lost sheep (15:1-7)
* the lost coin (15:8-10)
* the prodigal son (15:11-32)
* the Pharisee and the tax collector (18:9-14)
* Zacchaeus (19:1-10)
* the penitent thief (23:39-43).

Because of this emphasis on the forgiveness of sin, Luke's gospel is sometimes called the "Gospel of Mercy" (cf. Lk 6:36: "Be merciful, as your heavenly Father is merciful"). The same theme is frequently repeated in Luke's second book, the Acts (cf. 2:38; 3:19; 5:31; 8:22; 10:43; 11:18; 13:24; 13:38; 17:30; 19:4; 20:21; 26:18; 26:20).

But the liberation that Jesus brings to the poor is, in Vincent's vision, integral. Consequently, he sends the Daughters of Charity to minister to the poor "spiritually and corporally."[6] He organizes the Ladies of Charity and the Confraternities of Charity to work toward the same end. He warns the members of the Congregation of the Mission, moreover, that they should not think of their mission in exclusively spiritual terms.[7] Rather, they too should

---

1. SV XI, 4-5.
2. SV XII, 190.
3. SV XII, 264.
4. SV XII, 270-71.
5. Cf. Fitzmyer, *Ibid.*, 223: "When Luke looks back at the Christ-event, another way in which he sums up its effect is 'the forgiveness of sins. . .' "
6. SV IX, 59; IX, 593; XI, 364; XI, 592.
7. SV XII, 87: "If there are any among us who think they are in the Congregation of the Mission to preach the gospel to the poor but not to comfort them, to supply their spiritual but not their

care for the sick, the foundlings, the insane, even the most abandoned.[1] In this way they will preach by both word and work. In this way too, their love will be both "affective and effective."[2]

These two dimensions of Jesus' mission often flow together in St. Vincent's writings; he sees evangelization and human promotion as mutually complementing one another. "In this vocation we are closely conformed to Our Lord Jesus Christ, who, it would seem, made it his principal task to assist and care for the poor: 'He sent me to preach good news to the poor.' And if somebody asked Our Lord 'Why did you come on earth?' (he would answer): 'To assist the poor.' 'For any other reason?' 'To assist the poor' . . . And so, are we not then most happy to be part of the Mission for the very same reason that moved God to become man?"[3]

3. Christ lives in the person of the poor [4]

While the Christ of St. Vincent remains "Lord" and "Son of God," he lives in the person of the poor. He continues to suffer in them.[5]

He says to the Daughters of Charity on February 13, 1646: "In serving the poor, you serve Jesus Christ. O my Daughters, how true that is! You serve Christ in the person of the poor. That's as true as the fact that we are here."[6] He frequently cites Mt 25:31-46 to reinforce the identification of Jesus with the poor:[7] "So this is what obliges you to serve them with respect, as your masters, and with devotion: that they represent for you the person of Our Lord, who said: 'Whatever you do for one of these, the least of my brethren, I will consider it as done to me.' "[8]

Because of this identification with Christ, the poor are our "lords and masters."[9] In drafting the rule for the Daughters, he writes that they should: ". . . love one another deeply, as sisters whom he has joined together with the bond of his love, and that they should cherish the poor as their masters, since

---

    temporal wants, I reply that we ought to assist them and have them assisted in every way, by ourselves and by others. . . . To do this is to preach the gospel by words and by works."
1. SV XI, 393.
2. SV IX, 475, 592, 599; XI, 40.
3. SV XI, 108.
4. On this same theme, cf. José-María Ibañez, "Le Pauvre, Icône de Jésus-Christ," in *Monsieur Vincent, Témoin de L'Evangile* (Toulouse, 1990) 155-68.
5. SV X, 680.
6. SV IX, 252; cf. X, 123.
7. Cf. IX, 252, 324, 454; X, 332; XIII, 788, 790, 806; XII, 88, 100.
8. SV X, 332; cf. also X, 679-80; XIII, 805-806.
9. Cf. SV, IX, 119; X, 332.

Our Lord is in them, and they in Our Lord."[1] He repeats the same theme to the priests and brothers of the Mission: "Let us go then, my brothers, and work with a new love in the service of the poor looking even for the most poor and the most abandoned, recognizing before God that they are our lords and masters and that we are unworthy to render them our small services."[2] The Christ of Vincent, his "lord and master," is therefore to be found in the sick, the prisoner, the galley-slave, the abandoned child, those ravaged by the religious wars of the day.[3]

This identification of Christ with the suffering neighbor is a prominent theme in Luke's Acts (9:4; 22:7; 26:14: "Saul, Saul, why do you persecute me?"). It is also related to the Pauline theme of the Body of Christ (Rom 12:5; 1 Cor 10:17; Col 1:18; Eph 4:4; 5:23), and the Johannine theme of the unity of love of God and love of neighbor (Jn 13:34-35; 1 Jn 2:7f.; 3:11, 16, 18, 23-24; 4:20-21; 5:1-2; 2 Jn 5-6).

4. Christ has a universal outlook

Jesus wished the gospel to be preached "even to the ends of the earth" (Acts 1:8; cf. Lk 24:47). Vincent gradually became convinced of this aspect of the mind of Christ.[4] "Our vocation, then, is to go, not into one parish, nor even to one diocese, but throughout the whole world. And to do what? To inflame the hearts of men and women, to do what the Son of God did. He came to cast fire upon the earth, to enflame it with his love."[5]

Beginning in 1648 with the mission to Madagascar, he begins to send the members of the Congregation to various parts of the world. "Behold the beautiful field which God is opening up to us in Madagascar, the Hebrides and elsewhere! Let us beg him to enkindle in our hearts a desire to serve him. Let us give ourselves to him to do whatever he pleases with us."[6] Before the end of his life, Vincent also saw missionaries in Italy, Poland, Algeria, Tunis, and Ireland. He dreamed, as well, of sending them (or of going himself!) to the Indies.

Though this missionary work resulted in huge difficulties and loss of life, Vincent remained utterly convinced of its importance and, in the face of much opposition, defended it as the mind of Christ. "Some members of the

1. SV XIII, 540.
2. SV XI, 393.
3. SV X, 680.
4. SV XI, 257.
5. SV XII, 262.
6. SV XI, 74-75.

Company may say perhaps that Madagascar should be abandoned; flesh and blood will speak that language and say that no more men should be sent there, but I am certain that the Spirit says otherwise. . . . It would be quite some Company, that of the Mission, if, because five or six had died, it were to abandon the work of the Lord!"[1]

Once again, Vincent incorporates into his vision a strong Lucan theme, the universality of Christ's vision. In Luke's gospel, it is not just to his own that Christ has come, but to all the nations:

* Jesus is a light to illumine the gentiles (2:32)
* all humankind shall see the salvation of our God (3:6)
* there is more faith among the gentiles than in Israel (4:25-27)
* go along the streets and along the hedges and force them to enter (14:23)
* in his name conversion will be preached to all the nations (24:47)

This theme, sometimes called the "Gospel of Universal Salvation," is continued in Luke's second book, the Acts, where the disciples witness to the good news "in Jerusalem, in all Judea and Samaria, and even to the ends of the world" (Acts 1:8).

5. Christ is characterized by five missionary virtues:[2] simplicity, humility, meekness, mortification, and zeal.

In his important conference of August 22, 1659, St. Vincent focuses on these five virtues, which flow from the evangelical maxims, whose "author, who is Our Lord Jesus Christ . . . observed them."[3] He tells the members of the Congregation of the Mission that these five virtues are to be "the faculties of the soul of the entire Congregation."[4] In his conferences to the Daughters of Charity, he likewise focuses on simplicity and humility, in addition to charity itself. I will treat these five missionary virtues in much more detail in the next chapter. Here I will touch on them only briefly, as St. Vincent saw them in Christ.

a. The spirit of Jesus Christ[5] is one of simplicity, which consists in

---

1. SV XI, 420ff.; cf. also XI, 203-204, 402.
2. SV XII, 302: "Look at the force and power of the evangelical maxims, among which, since they are many in number, I have chosen principally those which are more proper to missionaries." Besides looking at the events in the life of Jesus, St. Vincent sees in the New Testament a series of maxims or sayings, of which Jesus is the "author." He asks his followers to do what Jesus did and to practice what he taught, either by direct command or through these maxims.
3. SV XII, 299.
4. CR II, 14; SV XII, 309.
5. SV IV, 486.

speaking the truth,[1] in saying things as they are,[2] without concealing or hiding anything,[3] and in referring things to God alone.[4] St. Vincent is so convinced of its importance that he calls simplicity "my gospel,"[5] "the virtue I love most."[6] "Do you know where Our Lord dwells?" he asks the Daughters of Charity. "It is among the simple."[7]

Vincent emphasizes here a central New Testament theme: Jesus' dedication to truth. John's gospel in particular focuses on this characteristic of Christ:

* Jesus is the truth (4:6)
* those who act in the truth come into the light (3:21)
* the truth sets you free (8:32)
* Jesus testifies to the truth (18:37)
* anyone who is of the truth hears his voice (18:37)

Besides these and other Johannine texts (cf. Jn 1:17; 4:24; 5:33; 14:6; 16:13; 17:17), the New Testament accents dedication to the truth as a moral imperative based on a saying of the Lord that appears in several contexts: "Say *yes* when you mean *yes* and *no* when you mean *no*" (Mt 5:37; cf. Jas 5:12; 2 Cor 1:17-20).

b. Humility, the virtue of Jesus Christ,[8] which he teaches us "by word and example,"[9] entails the recognition that all good comes from God.[10] It involves an acknowledgement of our own lowliness and faults,[11] accompanied by exuberant confidence in God.[12] Vincent urges the Company, above all, to consider "that admirable model of humility, Our Lord Jesus Christ."[13] He marveled how the Son of God "emptied himself" (Phil 2:7).[14]

While humility is emphasized by the other evangelists (cf. Mt 20:28; Mk 9:35; Jn 13:12-15), as well as by Paul (cf. Phil 2:5-11), it is a particularly emphatic Lucan theme, connected with the coming of salvation to the poor. Beginning with the infancy narratives, Luke depicts the advent of Jesus among the humble. God "looked upon his servant in her lowliness" (Lk 1:48).

---

1. CR II, 4; SV XII, 172.
2. SV I, 144.
3. SV I, 284; V, 464.
4. CR II, 4; SV, 172.
5. SV IX, 606.
6. SV I, 284.
7. SV X, 96.
8. SV XI, 56-57.
9. CR II, 7.
10. SV I, 182; VII, 98-99.
11. CR II, 7.
12. SV III, 279; V, 165.
13. SV XI, 394.
14. SV XII, 109; cf. Dodin, *op. cit.*, 37.

He "deposed the mighty from their thrones and raised the lowly to high places" (1:52). "For everyone who exalts himself shall be humbled and he who humbles himself shall be exalted" (14:11; cf. also 18:14). Jesus reminds his disciples that the truly great are those who become the least (22:26) and that he is in their midst "as the one who serves . . ." (22:27). Luke also develops the theme of exaltation through humiliation (cf. 9:22; 12:50; 24:7, 26, 46). In the Book of the Acts, he repeats that this is the key to understanding the scriptures (Acts 8:26-40).

c. Jesus himself tells us that he is meek, St. Vincent writes.[1] This virtue, for St. Vincent, is the ability to handle anger[2] either by suppressing it[3] or by expressing it,[4] in a manner governed by love.[5] It is approachability and affability.[6] It combines gentleness and firmness.[7] St. Vincent writes to St. Louise de Marillac on November 1, 1637: "If the gentleness of your spirit needs a dash of vinegar, borrow a little of it from the spirit of Our Lord. O, Mademoiselle, how very well he knew how to find a bitter-sweet remark when it was needed."[8]

It is Matthew's gospel that Vincent usually quotes when speaking of Jesus' meekness (Mt 11:29; cf. also 5:5; 21:5). But while Luke never uses the word "meekness" itself, the theme is so characteristic of the third gospel that Dante once described Luke as "the scribe of the gentleness of Christ."[9] Jesus' mercy (Lk 7:36ff.), his love (15:1ff.), his gracious words (4:22), and his joy (10:21) in Luke's gospel soften the starker portrait painted by Mark.

d. Jesus is the exemplar of mortification. "Let us never lose sight of the mortification of Our Lord, seeing that, to follow him, we are obliged to mortify ourselves after his example."[10] Vincent defines mortification as the subjection of passion to reason.[11] It finds a very prominent place in his conferences. To motivate his communities to engage in it, he cites many of the New Testament sayings recommending it.[12]

Once again the reader will note that this is a prominent Lucan theme:

* the disciples leave everything and follow Jesus (5:11)

---

1. CR II, 6.
2. SV XII, 186.
3. SV XII, 187.
4. SV XII, 187.
5. SV XII, 188.
6. SV XII, 189.
7. SV VII, 226.
8. SV I, 393-94.
9. *De monarchia* l.18.
10. SV XII, 227.
11. SV X, 56.
12. Cf. SV IX, 170; X, 61; X, 398.

* they must take up their cross daily (9:23)
* no one should put his hand to the plow and turn back (9:62)
* they should sell everything and give it as alms (12:33)
* they must hate father, mother, wife, children, brothers, sisters, even their very life (14:26)
* they must renounce everything (14:33)
* Jesus must suffer much before the reign of God is established (17:25)
* it was necessary that he be crucified (24:7)
* the Christ had to suffer in order to enter his glory (24:26)
* he must suffer and rise (24:46)

Because of this, Luke's gospel has sometimes been called the "Gospel of Absolute Renunciation."

e. Zeal is the burning love that fills the heart of Jesus. "Let us ask God to give the Company this spirit, this heart, this heart which will make us go everywhere, this heart of the Son of God, the heart of Our Lord . . . which will dispose us to go as he went and as he would have gone if his eternal wisdom had judged it fitting to labor for the conversion of those poor nations."[1] This fire of love enables the missionary to go anywhere and to do everything.[2] "The love of Christ drives us on" (2 Cor 5:14) becomes the motto of the Daughters of Charity.

Zeal is the virtue of missionary action. "If the love of God is the fire, zeal is its flame. If love is the sun, then zeal is its ray."[3] It aims "at extending the kingdom of God."[4] It is love in practice. "Let us love God, my brothers," Vincent de Paul cries out to the missionaries, "let us love God, but let it be with the strength of our arms and the sweat of our brows. So very often many acts of love of God, of resting in his presence, of benevolence, and such interior affections and practices, although very good and very desirable, are nevertheless to be suspected if they do not reach the practice of effective love."[5]

Practical love, on fire with spreading the kingdom of God, is of course central to the New Testament. It is also the quality for which Vincent de Paul is best known and in the service of which he organized so many men and women. One could cite many New Testament texts (cf. Mt 25:31-46; Rom 13:8; 1 Cor 13:13) focusing on its importance. Perhaps clearest of all are those in the Johannine corpus (cf. Jn 3:16; 13:34-35; 1 Jn 2:10; 3:11; 3:16; 3:18; 3:23; 4:7-8; 4:11; 4:19-21; 5:1-2).

---

1. SV XI, 291.
2. SV XI, 204: "Yes, the Congregation of the Mission can do all things because we have within us the germ of the omnipotence of Jesus Christ. . . ."
3. SV XII, 307-308; XII, 262.
4. SV XII, 307.
5. SV XI, 40.

6. Christ is constantly before the Father in prayer

Jesus' psychology, St. Vincent writes with precision in one of his letters, is caught up in two all-consuming directions, "his filial relationship with the Father and his charity toward the neighbor."[1] In the midst of his missionary activity, Jesus is always united with his Father (cf. Jn 7:29, 33:17, 13, 18).[2] He recognizes that the Father is the author of all the good that he does[3] and he constantly seeks his will.

In that light, St. Vincent tells the Daughters of Charity, ". . . Our Lord was, above all, a man of prayer."[4] In his Rule for the missionaries, he states: "Although we cannot perfectly imitate Christ our Lord who spent whole nights in prayer to God in addition to his daily meditations, nevertheless we will do so as far as we are able."[5]

Vincent is utterly convinced of the importance of the union of action and contemplation that he sees in Christ. He tells his followers that vocational stability and the ongoing vitality of their works depends on prayer.[6] He alludes repeatedly to a distinctively Lucan theme: that Jesus prays again and again, in the morning, at night, and on all the important occasions in his ministry:

* at his baptism (3:21)
* he withdraws to pray alone (5:16)
* he prays before he chooses the twelve (6:12)
* he prays before Peter's confession (9:18)
* he prays before the transfiguration (9:29)
* he tells them to pray for laborers for the harvest (10:2)
* he teaches the disciples to pray (11:1)
* he teaches them perseverance in prayer (18:1)
* he teaches them humility in prayer (18:9)
* he prays at the Last Supper, to strengthen Peter's faith (22:32)
* he prays during his agony in the garden (22:41-42)
* he prays on the cross (23:46)

In this sense, Luke's gospel is the "Gospel of Prayer." Luke's Book of the

---

1. SV VI, 393. The French reads: ". . . religion vers son Père."
2. Jesus' special relationship with his Father is also a Lucan theme; cf. 2:49; 3:22, 9:35; 10:21-22; 23:46.
3. SV XII, 109.
4. SV IX, 415.
5. CR X, 7.
6. SV XI, 83: "Give me a man of prayer and he will be capable of everything. He may say with the apostle, 'I can do all things in him who strengthens me.' The Congregation will last as long as it faithfully carries out the practice of prayer, which is like an impregnable rampart shielding the missionaries from all manner of attack." Cf. also SV III, 535; IX, 416; X, 583.

Acts continues this theme (cf. Acts 1:14; 1:24; 2:42; 3:1; 4:24; 4:31; 6:4; 9:11; 10:2-4; 10:9; 10:24; 10:30; 12:5; 12:12; 13:3; 14:23; 20:36; 21:5; 24:14).

7. Christ shares his life with many others and engages them in his ministry

St. Vincent establishes communities, after the example of Christ, "who assembled his apostles and disciples,"[1] for the sake of an apostolic mission.[2] Believing that "love is inventive, even to infinity,"[3] he founds the Congregation of the Mission and the Daughters of Charity. He organizes the Ladies of Charity and the Confraternities of Charity. He brings together men and women, rich and poor, learned and unlearned—all in the service of the poor.

He recognizes that women play a particularly prominent role in the ministry of Jesus.[4] The same becomes true in his own life: Marguerite Naseau,[5] Louise de Marillac,[6] Jane Frances de Chantal,[7] Madame de Gondi,[8] to name just the most prominent. This, too, is a distinctively Lucan theme. Luke, more than any of the other gospel writers, emphasizes the important place that women have in the life and ministry of Jesus:

* Mary, Elizabeth and Anna, in the infancy narratives
* the sinful woman (7:36-50)
* the women who accompany him (8:1-3)
* the widow of Naim (7:11-17)
* the woman who praises his mother (11:27-28)
* Martha and Mary (10:38-42)
* the women on the road to Calvary (23:27-31)
* the women who follow him to the end (23:55)
* the witnesses to his resurrection (24:22)

---

1. CR VIII, 1.
2. Cf. SV XIII, 197-98; 423.
3. SV XI, 146.
4. SV IX, 208-209, 456, 601; XIII, 455, 809-10; XIV, 125-26.
5. SV IX, 77.
6. Cf. X, 709; XIII, 695.
7. SV XIII, 125.
8. SV III, 399.

8. Christ trusts in the providence of his Father and exercises a providential care over the lives of his followers

While many of St. Vincent's conferences and writings speak of the providence of *God* (implicitly, and sometimes explicitly, the Father[1]), many others speak of *Christ's* providence for his followers.[2] In a letter to Bernard Codoing he emphasizes the former: "The rest will come in its time. Grace has its moments. Let us abandon ourselves to the providence of God and be very careful not to run ahead of it. If it pleases God to give me some consolation in our vocation it is this. That I think, so it seems to me, that we have tried to follow his great providence in everything. . . ."[3] Likewise he writes to St. Louise de Marillac: "My God, my daughter, what great hidden treasures there are in holy providence and how marvelously Our Lord is honored by those who follow it and do not kick against it!"[4]

Speaking of the providence which Jesus himself has for his followers, St. Vincent tells Jean Martin in 1647: "So, Father, let us ask Our Lord that everything might be done in accordance with his providence, that our wills be submitted to him in such a way that between him and us there might be only one, which will enable us to enjoy his unique love in time and in eternity."[5] In another letter to the impetuous Bernard Codoing in 1644 he states: "The consolation that Our Lord gives me is to think that, by the grace of God, we have always tried to follow and not run ahead of providence, which knows so wisely how to lead everything to the goal that Our Lord destines for it."[6] Three months later he adds: "But what are we going to do, you say? We will do what Our Lord wills, which is to keep ourselves always in dependence on his providence. . . ."[7]

One might argue that this, too, is a Lucan emphasis.[8] The Spirit of the Father and of Jesus is active from the beginning in Luke, guiding the course of history. He anoints Jesus with power from on high and directs him in his ministry.

* the Holy Spirit will come down on you and the power of the Most High will overshadow you (1:35)

* having received baptism . . . the Holy Spirit descended on him (3:22)

---

1. Cf. SV II, 473; III, 188; V, 396; VIII, 152.
2. This may not always be an intentional distinction since in Vincent's writings sometimes the actions of the Father are not clearly distinguished from those of the Son.
3. SV II, 453.
4. SV I, 68; cf. III, 197.
5. SV III, 197.
6. SV II, 456.
7. SV II, 469.
8. Cf. J. Schultz, "Gottes Vorsehung bei Lukas," *ZNTW* 54 (1963), 104-16.

* Jesus, filled with the Holy Spirit . . . was led by the Spirit into the desert (4:1)
* Jesus returned to Galilee with the power of the Holy Spirit (4:14)
* the Spirit of the Lord is upon me (4:18)
* Jesus rejoiced in the Holy Spirit (10:21)
* your heavenly Father will give the Holy Spirit to those who ask him (11:13)
* whoever blasphemes against the Holy Spirit will not be forgiven (12:10)
* the Holy Spirit will teach you at that moment what you should say (12:12)

The Book of Acts continues this theme of the "Gospel of the Holy Spirit." The Spirit energizes and guides the Church in its apostolic mission.[1]

CONCLUSION

Vincent de Paul's vision of Christ is an original one.[2] For him, Christ is most of all the Evangelizer of the Poor. He is a missionary Christ, coming from the Father and returning to him, emptying himself of his condition as Son of God in order to free his people from the bondage, both corporal and spiritual, in which they are chained. He identifies with, and makes his home within, the poor themselves. His vision is universal, impelling him to preach the good news to the poor even to the ends of the earth. This Christ draws others together, male and female, rich and poor, and forms them to share in his mission. The virtues that particularly characterize him are five missionary ones: simplicity, humility, meekness, mortification, and zeal. Even in the midst of great activity he stands before his Father constantly in prayer, seeking his will and trusting in his providence.

Need I add how strikingly contemporary is the vision of this seventeenth-century saint? Today we find Vincent's preferential love for the poor echoed in one contemporary Church document after another.[3] His stress on a broad concept of evangelization, including human promotion and liberation from various forms of human bondage, or what Vincent calls "serving the poor

---

1. There are fifty-seven references to the Spirit in Acts; cf. Fitzmyer, *Ibid.*, 227.
2. One might, of course, add other elements in St. Vincent's vision of Christ (Christ as priest, Christ as living in poverty, chastity and obedience, etc.). In this article, I have focused only those which seem to me most characteristic of St. Vincent's vision.
3. Cf., among many other texts, *Redemptoris Mater* 37; Congregazione per la Dottrina della Fede, *Istruzione su "Libertà cristiana e liberazione"* (March 22, 1986) 68; *Sollicitudo Rei Socialis* 42.

both corporally and spiritually," are the centerpiece of the modern social encyclicals and numerous other episcopal and papal writings.[1] The importance of lay involvement in ministry and the need to revitalize ministerial formation both of the clergy and the laity are themes that resonate throughout the Church.[2] Renewed interest in apostolic spirituality and prayer is one of the signs of the times today.[3]

In what ways will contemporary Christology pursue the path along which this wonderfully realistic man walked: focusing on Christ as the Evangelizer of the Poor? How will it further articulate, and concretize, the ramifications of his vision? That is surely the contemporary challenge.

---

1. Cf. Congregazione per la Dottrina della Fede, *Istruzione su "Libertà cristiana e liberazione"* (March 22, 1986) 97; *Sollicitudo Rei Socialis* 46.
2. Cf. Synod of Bishops 1987, "Message to the People of God" 12; *Sollicitudo Rei Socialis* 47.
3. Cf. Donald Dorr, *Spirituality and Justice* (Dublin: Gill and Macmillan, 1984) 21-22.

Chapter II

FIVE CHARACTERISTIC VIRTUES: YESTERDAY AND TODAY

... we should look on them as the five smooth stones with which, even at the first assault, we will defeat the infernal Goliath in the name of the Lord of Armies ...

CR XII, 12

I write this chapter with some hesitation, knowing that the task I am undertaking is a difficult, even if very important, one. For Vincent de Paul, simplicity, humility, meekness, mortification, and zeal were the characteristic virtues of a missionary. He saw them as "the five smooth stones by which we might conquer the evil Goliath." These virtues are so central to St. Vincent's thinking that in efforts at renewal all those who share in the Vincentian tradition must grapple with their meaning and the forms they might take in the modern world.

This chapter is divided into three parts: 1) a study of the five characteristic virtues as St. Vincent himself understood them; 2) a brief description of horizon-shifts that have taken place in theology and spirituality between the seventeenth and twentieth centuries; 3) an attempt at retrieving the five virtues in contemporary forms.

I offer the research and theological reflection in this chapter especially to the members of the Congregation of the Mission and the Daughters of Charity, but also to the many other groups of priests, sisters, brothers and lay men and women who walk in the spirit of Vincent de Paul. I hope that it will help in their efforts at ongoing renewal. I recognize the limitations of what I have written in the third part of the chapter. I trust that through dialogue the reflections that I have sketched there will be supplemented.

I - THE FIVE CHARACTERISTIC VIRTUES
AS TAUGHT BY ST. VINCENT[1]

1. Simplicity

a. For St. Vincent, simplicity is first of all, speaking the truth (CR II, 4; XII, 172). It is saying things as they are (I, 144), without concealing or hiding anything (I, 284; V, 464). He expresses this in a letter to François du Coudray on November 6, 1634:

> You know that your own kind heart has given me, thanks be to God, full liberty to speak to you with the utmost confidence, without any concealment or disguise; and it seems to me that up to the present you have recognized that fact in all my dealings with you. My God! Am I to fall into the misfortune of being forced to do or to say in my dealings with you anything contrary to holy simplicity? Oh! Sir! May God preserve me from doing so in regard to anything whatsoever! It is the virtue I love most, the one to which in all my actions I pay most heed, so it seems to me; and if it were lawful to say so, the one, I may say, in which I have, by God's mercy, made some progress (I, 284).

The heart must not think one thing while the mouth says another (IX, 81; IX, 605; XII, 172). The missionary must avoid all duplicity, dissimulation, cunning, and double meaning (II, 340; IX, 81).

> For myself, I don't know, but God gives me such a great esteem for simplicity that I call it my gospel. I have a particular devotion and consolation in saying things as they are. (IX, 606)

b. Simplicity also consists in referring things to God alone (CR II, 4), or purity of intention (XII, 172). In this sense simplicity is doing everything for love of God and for no other end (XII, 174; XII, 302; II, 315). It entails

---

1. The author apologizes for the somewhat tedious, and at times schematic, treatment of what St. Vincent taught about the five virtues. I have attempted to give a complete account here of all that St. Vincent wrote and said on the subject, as found mainly in P. Coste's fourteen volumes, supplemented principally by A. Dodin, as well as by several others. It seems to me that a foundational study of this sort is utterly necessary as one attempts to recapture these virtues in contemporary forms. All references in the first part of this chapter are to Coste's edition, unless otherwise noted, and are designated *SV*. References to the Common Rules of the Congregation of the Mission are designated *CR*. For some interesting information on this same subject, as well as further bibliography, the reader may wish to consult: J.-P. Renouard, "L'Esprit de la Congrégation: Les Vertus Fondamentales," *Vincentiana* XXVIII (1984) 599-615; cf. also T. Davitt, "The Five Characteristic Virtues," *Colloque XIV* (Autumn 1986) 109-120. Cf. also Christian Sens, "Comme Prêtre Missionaire," in *Monsieur Vincent, Témoin de L'Evangile* (Toulouse, 1990) 133-151, esp. 140f.

avoiding "human respect" (II, 340). The missionary must never do good acts in one place in order to be recommended for an assignment in another place (II, 314).

c. Simplicity involves an unadorned lifestyle. We fail against simplicity, St. Vincent tells us, when our rooms are filled with superfluous furniture, pictures, large numbers of books, and vain and useless things (XII, 175). We must use with great simplicity the things that have been given to us (IX, 607).

d. For the missionary, simplicity also entails explaining the gospel by familiar comparisons (XI, 50), using the Little Method that was employed in the Congregation of the Mission at that time (CR XII, 5): preaching about a virtue, for example, by presenting:
- motives for living it,
- its nature or definition, and
- means for putting it into practice (SV XI, 260).

e. In St. Vincent's mind, simplicity was very closely linked with humility (I, 144) and it was inseparable from prudence (CR II, 5), which for him meant always basing one's judgment on the evangelical maxims or on the judgments of Jesus Christ (XII, 169; XII, 176). Both prudence and simplicity tend toward the same goal: to speak and to act well (XII, 176).

f. St. Vincent gives a whole series of motives as to why his double family should practice simplicity:
- God communicates with the simple (CR II, 4; II, 341; XII, 170; XII, 302).
- God himself is simple; so where simplicity is there God is too (XI, 50).
- The world loves simple people (XII, 171).
- Missionaries especially ought to love it (XII, 302), since it will help them in dealing with simple people.
- It is the spirit of Jesus Christ (IV, 486).
- God wants the Community to have this virtue (XII, 303), especially since it lives in a world that is filled with duplicity.
- Duplicity is never agreeable to God (IV, 486).
- It is the simple who keep the true religion (XII, 171).

g. St. Vincent also lists means by which simplicity is acquired:
- It is obtained by frequent acts (XII, 181).
- We should say everything openly to our superiors, without trying to hide what is embarrassing to us (IX, 606; X, 64; X, 96; X, 146; X, 355).
- We should obey the rule to please God, not the superior (IX, 444).
- We should carry out orders without asking why (IX, 605).

2. Humility

a. Humility, for St. Vincent, is the recognition that all good comes from God. He writes to Firmin Get on March 8, 1658: "*Let us no longer say: it is I who have done this good work; for every good thing ought to be done in the name of our Lord Jesus Christ . . .*" (VII, 98-99). "*Be very much on your guard against attributing anything to yourself. By doing so you would commit robbery and do injury to God, who alone is the author of every good thing,*" he writes to Jacque Pesnelle on October 15, 1658 (VII, 289). God pours out his abundant gifts on the humble "*who recognize that all good which is done by them comes from God*" (I, 182).

b. Humility is recognition of our own lowliness and faults (CR II, 7), accompanied by exuberant confidence in God (III, 279; V, 165; II, 233; II, 336; X, 201; IX, 382). In writing to Charles Nacquart on March 22, 1648 about the gift of vocation, he states: "*Humility alone is capable of receiving this grace. A perfect abandonment of everything that you are and can be in the exuberant confidence in your sovereign creator ought to follow*" (III, 279).

Our sins too should help us grow in humility (XI, 397).

c. Humility involves voluntary self-emptying (V, 534; XI, 61; XI, 312; XII,200). This entails loving to be unknown and abandoned (VII, 312; X, 129; X, 152; XII, 709). It means avoiding the applause of the world (I, 496; IX, 605; X,148). It involves taking the last place (IX, 605) and loving the hidden life (IX, 680).

d. Humility involves esteeming others as more worthy than yourself (V, 37; IX, 303). In this regard, it is a communal virtue not just an individual one. We are to regard the Company as the least of all (IX, 303; X, 200; XI, 60; XI, 114-15; XI, 434; XII, 438).

e. St. Vincent gives numerous motives for the practice of humility:

- He notes that Jesus was humble and happy to be seen as the least of men (I, 182; I, 534; XI, 400).
- It is the characteristic virtue of Jesus (XI, 400), and should be the characteristic virtue of the Congregation of the Mission (XI, 57): "*Grant that humility may be the characteristic virtue of the Mission! Oh holy virtue, how beautiful you are. O little Company, how lovable you will be if God grants you this grace*" (XII, 204). It is also the characteristic virtue of a true Daughter of Charity (X, 527).
- Saints too were humble: "*It is the virtue of Jesus Christ, the virtue of his holy mother, the virtue of the greatest of the saints, and finally it is the virtue of missionaries*" (XI, 56-57).

- God blesses humble beginnings (II, 281; V, 487).
- Humility is the origin of all the good that we do (IX, 674).
- God has called us, lowly people, to do great things (X, 128; X, 198).
- It is the arms by which we conquer the devil (I, 536; XI, 312), since the devil and pride are the same (IX, 706).
- We cannot persevere without humility (I, 528; X, 528; XII, 304).
- It brings all other virtues with it (XII, 210).
- It is the foundation of all evangelical perfection, the node of the whole spiritual life (CR II, 7).
- Everyone loves it (XII, 197), but it is easier to think about than to practice (XI, 54).
- It is the source of peace and union (XII, 106; XII, 210).
- If the Company possesses humility, it will be a paradise: "*If you establish yourselves in it, what will happen? You will make of this Company a paradise and people will likely say that it is a group of the happiest people on earth . . .*" (X, 439).
- Heaven is won by humility (CR II, 6).
f. St. Vincent suggested many means for acquiring humility:
  - We should do acts of humility daily (IX, 680; XII, 716; I, 183).
  - We should confess our faults openly (V, 164; XI, 54) and accept the admonitions of others (CR X, 13-14).
  - We should desire to be admonished (IX, 382).
  - We should pray to our Lord and the Blessed Mother as models of humility (IX, 680; XI, 56-57).
  - We should believe that we are the worst in the world (X, 552).
  - We should recognize that everyone has his faults; then there will be little trouble excusing others (X, 438).
  - We should preach Jesus Christ and not ourselves (XII, 22).
  - Superiors should so act that others will not be able to tell that they are superiors (XI, 346; IX, 302).

3. Meekness

What St. Vincent teaches about meekness is most clearly delineated in a conference given on March 28, 1659. We also owe much to his letters to Louise de Marillac, to whom he often speaks about combining meekness with strength.

a. Meekness is the ability to handle anger (XII, 186). One can do this either by suppressing it (XII, 186) or by expressing it (XII, 187), governed by love (XII, 188).

b. Meekness is also approachability, gentleness, affability, and serenity of countenance toward those who approach us (XII, 189).

c. It entails enduring offenses with forgiveness and courage. We should treat gently even those who do injury to us (XII, 191). *"Meekness makes us not only excuse the affronts and injustices we receive, but even inclines us to treat with gentleness those from whom we receive them, by means of kind words, and should they go so far as to abuse us and even strike us on the face, it makes us endure all for God. Such are the effects produced by this virtue. Yes, a servant of God who truly possesses it, when violent hands are laid upon him, offers to the divine goodness this rough treatment and remains in peace"* (XII, 192).

d. It is based on respect for the person (IX, 269).

e. It involves combining gentleness and firmness. He writes to Louise de Marillac on November 1, 1637: *"If the meekness of your spirit needs a drop of vinegar, borrow a little of it from the spirit of our Lord. Oh, Mademoiselle, how very well he knew how to find the bitter-sweet when it was necessary"* (I, 393-94). To Denis Laudin, superior at Mans, he writes on August 7, 1658: *"Bear with him, therefore, Monsieur, but make him keep the rule as much as you can, according to the spirit of our Lord who is equally gentle and firm. If a man is not won over by meekness and patience, it will be difficult to win him over in any other way."* (VII, 226)

f. St. Vincent offers many motives to the double family for practicing humility:

- He tells them that our Lord is eternal meekness toward us (IV, 53; I, 341; IX, 266).

- *"There are no persons more constant and firm in doing good than those who are meek and gracious. While on the contrary, those who allow themselves to yield to anger and to passions of the irascible appetite are usually more inconstant, because they act only by fits and starts. They are like torrents, which are strong and impetuous only when in full flood but which dry up immediately afterwards, while rivers, which represent the meek and gracious, flow on noiselessly, tranquilly and unfailingly"* (XI, 65).

- Where Daughters of Charity live in respect and meekness, it is paradise; it is hell where they do not (IX, 268).

- Charity consists of love and meekness (IX, 267); if a sister is not meek, then she is not a Daughter of Charity (IX, 268).

- Meekness disposes people to turn to the Lord (CR II, 6).

- Heretics, galley slaves, and those fallen away are won over by patience and cordiality (IV, 53; IV, 120; XI, 66; IV, 449; I, 341). Disputation

does not aim at truth but at resisting the arguments of others, whereas meekness aims at the truth (XI, 65).
- A missionary needs meekness if he is to be able to endure the roughness of poor people (XII, 305).

g. St. Vincent suggests many means for acquiring meekness:
- He tells the Company that the contrary vice can be overcome if one works at it, as he himself had to do (IX, 64).
- Before speaking or deciding or acting, the angry person should hold his tongue and cool down (XI, 67).
- We should refrain from invective, reproach and rough words (IV, 53).
- We should not speak too loudly, but modestly and gently (IX, 274).
- We should ask pardon readily (IX, 275).
- We should learn, like St. Augustine, when to tolerate evil rather than try to abolish all evil practices (IV, 121).
- We should learn to submit our judgments to others (XII, 318).

4. Mortification

St. Vincent has a very developed teaching concerning mortification which he explains in numerous conferences, particularly to the Daughters of Charity.

a. Mortification entails denial of the exterior senses: sight, smell, taste, touch, and hearing (IX, 23; X, 59; X, 151; X, 246; X, 280; X, 399; XII, 215). He gives many examples in this regard. The Daughters of Charity, for example, should look at men only if this is necessary or useful. They should not be looking all around, but should keep their eyes moderately low (although service of the poor demands that they maintain a cheerful appearance). They should learn to endure bad smells especially when they are with the sick poor. They should mortify taste by not eating between meals. They should also eat foods which are not pleasing to them. They should not listen to gossip. They should not touch the neighbor nor allow themselves to be touched.

b. Mortification also involves denial of the interior senses: understanding, memory and will (X, 151; X, 246; X, 280). They should not want to know all sorts of curious things (*scientia inflat*). Nor should they be conjuring up, in their memories, pleasures that they had with their families, their romances, the caresses of their parents, etc. They should seek to come to a state of complete indifference, desiring only to do the will of God.

c. It entails denial of the passions of the soul. There are eleven of these, according to St. Vincent, of which love/hate and hope/despair are the most important (X, 248).

d. Basically, for St. Vincent, mortification is the subjection of passion to reason (X, 56). A person has a lower and a higher part. The lower part makes him like an animal; the higher part tends toward God (X, 55). The lower wants to revolt against the higher (X, 56; X, 244-45).

e. Mortification aims at indifference (X, 282), detachment (XII, 20). It is a continual struggle, but the struggle does get easier as time goes on (X, 251; XII, 226).

f. St. Vincent proposes many motives to his double family for practicing mortification:

- He quotes scripture passages recommending mortification: Matthew 16:24; Luke 14:26; Matthew 10:37; Romans 8:13; 2 Corinthians 4:10 (IX, 170; X, 61; X, 398).
- Jesus did only the will of his Father, constantly mortifying himself (XII, 214): "*Gentlemen, let us keep this example before our eyes. Let us never lose sight of the mortification of our Lord, seeing that, to follow him, we are obligated to mortify ourselves after his example. Let us model our affections upon his, that his footsteps may be the guide of ours in the ways of perfection. The saints are saints because they walk in his footsteps, renounce themselves, and mortify themselves in all things*" (XII, 227).
- He tells them that, in the long run, it is necessary to suffer, so they should be sure to make good use of suffering (X, 186-87).
- He points out that the lives of some, like M. Pillé, are a perpetual mortification (II, 342).
- Mortification of the senses helps us in prayer (X, 279; IX, 427).
- Mortification and prayer are two sisters who always go together: "*Mortification is another means, my daughters, which will be of great help to you on the road to prayer. Prayer and mortification are two sisters who are so closely united together that one will never be found without the other. Mortification goes first and prayer follows after, so that, my dear daughters, if you wish to become daughters of prayer, as you should, learn to mortify yourselves*" (IX, 427).
- Mortification makes satisfaction for our sins (X, 61).
- It is not as demanding for a Daughter of Charity as for a Carmelite and others (X, 98).
- Many have lost their vocations because they failed to accept mortification from the hands of God (X, 186; XII, 320).
- If we do not continually work to get better, we will get worse; there is

no standing still (X, 245). Progress in the spiritual life depends on progress in mortification (XI, 70).

- It is a paradise on earth when we can accept mortification as coming from God (X, 284).
- To encourage the Company, St. Vincent tells the story of his own difficulty in separating himself from his relatives (XII, 219).

g. St. Vincent proposes a number of means for acquiring the habit of mortification:

- It is acquired little by little, through repeated acts: "*In regard to what you have proposed about working hard to mortify the judgment and the will of your seminarists*," St. Vincent writes to Pierre du Beaumont on October 3, 1655, "*I will say to you, Monsieur, that that cannot be done all at once, but little by little with meekness and patience. Mortification, like the other virtues, is acquired only by repeated acts*" (V, 436).
- It involves:
  * bearing with one another (IX, 176),
  * accepting inconveniences in the house (IX, 188-89),
  * checking our tongues (X, 403), and
  * being careful and reserved in dealing with members of the opposite sex (XII, 21; X, 60; X, 151).
- The Rule asks for mortification in regard to:
  1) will
  2) judgment
  3) senses
  4) relatives and parents (CR II, 8-9), and, in a conference to the Company given on May 2, 1659, he adds, citing St. Basil:
  5) pomp
  6) the desire to preserve yourself and live long (XII, 220-23), and
  7) putting off the old man and putting on the new (XII, 224).

h. St. Vincent encourages his confreres to practice mortifications, under the guidance of their superiors or directors, to the extent that their health and their labors permit. But because of their continual labors as missionaries he does not wish that the Rule burden them with mortifications and bodily austerities (CR X, 15).

5. Zeal

St. Vincent speaks less frequently in an explicit way about zeal. He touches on the subject in passing, however, and speaks about it eloquently on those occasions.

a. Zeal is love on fire. "*If love of God is the fire, zeal is its flame. If love is the sun, then zeal is its ray*" (XII, 307-08; XII, 262). "*Charity when it dwells in a soul takes complete possession of all its powers. It never rests. It is a fire that acts ceaselessly*" (XI, 216). It involves:

- a willingness to go anywhere to spread the reign of Christ: "*Let us ask God to give the Company this spirit, this heart, this heart which will make us go everywhere, this heart of the Son of God, the heart of our Lord, the heart of the Lord, the heart of the Lord [sic] which will dispose us to go as he went and as he would have gone if his eternal wisdom had judged it fitting to labor for the conversion of those poor nations. He sent his apostles to do that. He sends us, like them, to bear this divine fire everywhere, everywhere*" (XI, 291, cf. XI, 402; XII, 307);

- willingness to die for Christ: "*You see, gentlemen and my brothers, we should all have in ourselves the disposition and desire to suffer for God and for our neighbor and to wear ourselves out for that. Oh, how happy they are to whom God gives such dispositions and desires. Yes, gentlemen, we should be completely for God and for the service of the people. We should give ourselves to God to that end and wear ourselves out for that and give our lives to that end. We must strip ourselves bare, so to speak, in order to put on the new man. At least we should desire to be so disposed if we are not so already: to be ready and disposed to come and go according to God's pleasure, whether it be the Indies or elsewhere. Finally, we should be willing to devote ourselves to the service of our neighbor and to extend the rule of Jesus Christ in souls. And I myself, old and infirm as I am, should not cease to be disposed, yes, even to set out for the Indies to win souls for Christ, even if I should die on the way or aboard ship*" (XI, 402; cf. XI, 371; XI, 415).

b. It entails hard work for the salvation of our neighbor (XI, 444-45; XI, 307). "*Let us love God, my brothers, let us love God, but let it be with the strength of our arms and with the sweat of our brows. So very often many acts of love of God, of complacency, of benevolence, and such interior affection and practices, although very good and very desirable, are nevertheless to be suspected if they do not reach the practice of effective love*" (XI, 40).

c. It is to be contrasted with two extremes (CR XII, 11):

1) sloth, laxity, lack of fervor or sensitivity (XI, 193; XI, 17; XII, 321); and

2) indiscreet zeal (I, 96; I, 84; II, 140; X, 671).

The latter includes overwork (I, 84), unnecessarily exposing oneself or others to danger (IV, 121), being rigorous and overbearing with people as the young sometimes are (II, 70-71), and remaining too long with one sick person to the prejudice of another (X, 671). He urges Louise de Marillac (I, 96): "*Be very careful to conserve it (your health) for the love of the Lord and his poor members and be careful not to do too much. It is a ruse of the devil by which he deceives good souls when he incites them to do more than they can in order that they might not be able to do anything.*"

d. St. Vincent offers the double family several motives for zeal:
- He tells them that Jesus' love was so great that he was willing to die (XI, 415).
- The blood of Christians is the seed of Christianity (XI, 415).
- God allowed the deaths of many in the beginning of the Church (XI, 415, XI, 422).

e. He urges confreres to take the means to grow in zeal:
- He writes to François du Coudray: "*Picture to yourself then, sir, that there are millions of souls with outstretched hands calling you, saying: 'Ah, M. du Coudray, you who have been chosen from all eternity by the providence of God to be our second redeemer, have pity on us who grope in ignorance of the things necessary for our salvation in the sins that we have never dared to confess and who without your help will certainly be damned'*" (I, 252).
- He encourages M. Descart (II, 70-72) to grow in a charity that is nourished by experimental knowledge and that avoids rigor and excess.

PART II - HORIZON-SHIFTS IN THEOLOGY AND SPIRITUALITY BETWEEN THE SEVENTEENTH AND TWENTIETH CENTURIES

One could write extensively on this subject. Here I will offer merely a brief description of some horizon-shifts that have taken place between the seventeenth and twentieth centuries. Except for a few references to Church documents, I will not attempt to provide extensive documentation concerning these shifts, since I trust that the reader, whether he might react favorably or unfavorably to the shifts, will quickly recognize them as changes in thinking that have already taken place or are currently taking place. Only those horizon-shifts have been selected which have some impact on the way one views the five virtues.

1. A change in philosophical and theological methodology

The emphasis here has shifted from a classical to a more historical way of thinking.[1] The classicist mentality is deductive. It emphasizes universal principles and necessary conclusions. Working, for example, from the datum that Jesus is God, it draws necessary conclusions about his certain knowledge of future events. Over the centuries a detailed Christology "from above" has been worked out through a rigorous application of the deductive process. The method tends to be abstract and *a priori*. It examines the nature of things and draws conclusions in regard to particular instances depending on whether or not they correspond to the abstract nature. The method has been applied systematically to dogmatic, moral, and spiritual questions.

The historical mode of thinking emphasizes changing circumstances and contingent conclusions. It begins with concrete data, employs an empirical method, stresses hermeneutics, and draws its conclusions inductively from its sources. This historical way of thinking has brought in its wake numerous changes in liturgical matters like the reform of the sacrament of penance, the restoration of communion under both kinds, the reception of communion in the hand, the use of eucharistic ministers, etc. It also has had great influence in the development of Christology "from below," the question of religious liberty, and the contemporary discussion of many moral questions.

A significant consequence of this shift in emphasis in philosophical and theological methodology is that change has come to find a greater place in our expectations. People today are willing to accept fewer absolutes. They question absolute prohibitions which were formerly accepted. They em-

---

1. Cf. *Gaudium et Spes* 5.

48

phasize that changing circumstances make one case different from another.

Another consequence of this horizon-shift has been increasing pluralism. Contemporary thinkers recognize the value of different cultures, philosophies, and theologies. The inductive method emphasizes the *search for truth* rather than the *possession of truth*. An obvious sign of this in ecclesial matters is the ecumenical movement.

2. Increasing consciousness of interdependence

Communication has been the key in this regard.[1] When an event took place in the seventeenth century in Europe, it might take a year before the news reached the colonies in North and South America. Even more, many in the colonies never came to know of the event. In the twentieth century we know of events everywhere in the world seconds after they happen. Struggles in the Middle East have worldwide ramifications (e.g., because of the importance of oil throughout the world). People are increasingly conscious of their interdependence on one another.

An evident consequence of this change in horizon has been the emphasis on a global world view in the writings of John XXIII, Paul VI, and John Paul II. While patriotism, for example, is still seen as a virtue, exaggerated forms of nationalism are viewed as an enemy to global solidarity. Episcopal and papal writings emphasize universal brotherhood and sisterhood. Social encyclicals criticize the widening gap between the rich nations and the poor nations. Critical voices note that some are rich *because* others are poor.

This horizon-shift has had great ramifications in religious communities. Young people especially seek new forms of community where there is real communication. They spurn formalized structures that sometimes thwart communication while purporting to promote it. They expect shared responsibility. They look for communal forms of prayer which are alive and which do not smack of formalism.

In the secular and religious spheres, the global community has also grown in consciousness of the implications of the arms buildup. The sale of arms remains one of the major factors in the world economy. Concomitantly a series of local conflicts (Iran/Iraq, Israel/Lebanon, Ethiopia/Somalia, the Soviet invasion of Afghanistan, the US invasion of Panama, revolutionary movements in Central America, the Iraqi invasion of Kuwait, etc.) makes the international scene quite volatile, with the ever-present danger that these

---

1. Pastoral Instruction on the Means of Social Communication 6-7; Cf. John Naisbitt, *Megatrends* (New York, 1984) 14-15.

conflicts will escalate in an "all-out war" (as in the last instance). Young people attest to an uncertainty about their future because of the possibility of nuclear annihilation.

The United States Bishops' Peace Pastoral has set off a broad series of discussions on the question of war and peace among episcopal conferences throughout the world. Numerous papal statements have likewise addressed the subject.

3. A changed paradigm for the exercise of authority

There has been a shift from a monarchical model of authority to a collegial model. *Lumen Gentium* has made this shift a part of official Church thinking.[1]

The new paradigm brings with it new expectations: dialogue, questioning, shared decision-making, shared responsibility. It emphasizes that authority serves the community and seeks to empower the group and individuals within it.

This shift in horizon has also brought with it the current crisis of authority in the Church, as well as a crisis of authority in civil society. Dissent from official Church teaching has become fairly common (e.g., in regard to birth control). Civil unrest has become the inevitable response to governments that deny people a voice in regard to decisions affecting their future (resulting, for example, in an amazingly rapid change in the political situation of Eastern Europe, in ongoing turmoil in the Soviet Union, and in renewed oppression in China).

4. Emphasis on a Christology and an ecclesiology "from below"

This horizon-shift is related to the first and third shifts mentioned above.

The explosion in scriptural, linguistic, archaeological, and historical research in the nineteenth and twentieth centuries, as well as the development of hermeneutics, has led to a deeper understanding of the varying Christologies in the New Testament. These are often roughly grouped into the categories "from above" and "from below."

Different from the classical Christology, a Christology "from below" focuses on data about the humanity of Jesus, while also affirming his divinity. It accepts the scriptural data about his weakness, his lack of knowledge about the future, his ignorance of events outside the scope of his experience, his anger, his deep human love, his feelings, his emotions, etc.

---

1. *Lumen Gentium* 18-28.

An ecclesiology "from below" emphasizes base communities, the role of the lay person, shared decision-making and responsibility, varied ministries, the identification of the Church with the poor and their struggles, etc. Much of this shift in emphasis can be found in official Church documents such as those of Medellin and Puebla.[1]

5. A shift toward a more positive attitude in regard to creation and toward less emphasis on sin

The struggle with Jansenism greatly influenced seventeenth century thinking. Theologians and spiritual writers, while combatting Jansenism, were influenced by many of its presuppositions. It was "in the air they breathed," so to speak. Like Manicheanism and Albigensianism, two of its predecessors, it had a very negative view of created reality. It was overly rigorous. It focused on sin. The twentieth century has brought a renewed emphasis on the dignity of the human person and on the goodness of creation. This is particularly evident in *Gaudium et Spes*[2] and the writings of John Paul II.[3] Theologians and spiritual writers take a much more positive attitude toward "the human." The human person is seen as the center of creation. Created realities are extensions of his being and ways in which he celebrates and shares God's gifts.

The shadow side of this horizon-shift is that it has brought with it a deepening loss of the sense of sin. Consequently, among young people especially, there is a diminished consciousness of the need for mortification and penance. The twentieth century has witnessed increased sexual permissiveness in society and a weakening of family structures. In some parts of the world, one out of two marriages ends in divorce. The number of single-parent families is huge. In some cities more than half the children are born out of wedlock. The extended family and its tight network of relationships is becoming much less common. Abortion is widespread.

Moral attitudes toward sexual behavior have changed very significantly since the seventeenth century. In many societies, divorce is now widely accepted as a way of terminating marital commitment. Birth control and premarital sex are engaged in extensively and frequently accepted as morally legitimate. Beyond efforts at eliminating prejudice against homosexuals, there is considerable agitation to accept the homosexual lifestyle as an alternative one.

---

1. *Puebla* 188-197; 617-57.
2. *Gaudium et Spes* 9, 12, 22.
3. Cf. *Redemptor Hominis, passim.*

6. A shift from the "era of Christendom" to the "era of the secular"

"Christendom," where religious values and practice were reinforced by civic and societal structures, has gradually been disappearing. Church and state have become more and more separated. "Post-Christian" and "non-Christian" societies have developed.

Concomitantly, theology and spirituality emphasize a positive sense of the secular. Secular reality, as God's gift in creation, has an autonomy and value of its own.[1] It can be understood on its own terms. In ethical terms, what is truly human is perceived as a moral good. Consequently, what truly promotes humanity builds up the kingdom of God.

This shift in horizon has actually brought in its wake a movement toward unity in theological perspective. It displaces the "two-storied" approach to nature and grace. It sees them as coinciding in the concrete. It avoids the split between the religious sphere and the secular sphere or between religion and morality.

At the same time, however, on the negative side, the twentieth century has seen the widespread diffusion of "secularism" in the form of materialistic philosophies and attitudes. Marxism/communism came to dominate much of the world, even if today it finds itself in crisis. Capitalism too has had negative impact by its overemphasis on capital itself, productivity, and the amassing of material goods, with a consequent underemphasis on the human person and his or her labor, the universal destiny of material goods, the rights of the poor, etc.

In a rather unpublicized, but striking, way, there has also been a geographical shift of focus within the Church from the north to the south, away from the heartland of traditional "Christendom." This is what Walbert Buhlmann calls "the coming of the third Church."

By the year 2,000, there will be 153 million Catholics in Africa alone. The majority of Catholics will live in Latin America, Africa, and Southeast Asia. Among the peoples of these emerging nations, there is increasing emphasis on human rights, equality, and liberation. This is evident in the Puebla document and in the struggle of the churches of Latin America.

As a result of this horizon-shift, church life is strongly influenced by *comunidades de base*. Moral reflection emphasizes the need to liberate peoples from oppressive socio-economic structures. "Social sin" and "sinful structures" are much emphasized.

---

1. Cf. *Gaudium et Spes* 36.

PART III - THE FIVE VIRTUES RETRIEVED

The third part of this chapter will be an attempt at retrieving the values underlying the virtues which St. Vincent left to the communities that he inspired. Put in traditional terms, the object of this section will be to uncover the substance of the five virtues, to put aside those forms that are no longer appropriate to the modern world, and to suggest contemporary forms which the virtues might take. Naturally, not all of the forms which these virtues took in the seventeenth century are irrelevant today. Many still apply. On the other hand, some forms, and the language by which they are described, are no longer relevant because of changing times and circumstances. Other new forms have arisen which embody the substance of the five virtues.

1. Simplicity

In some ways simplicity is the easiest of the five virtues to retrieve. *Gandhi's Truth*,[1] as the title of Erik Erikson's psycho-biography puts it, speaks eloquently to young people in the modern world. The virtue which St. Vincent loved most, his "gospel," so to speak, still appeals. In a contemporary context, it can take many forms, some of which are suggested below.

a. Speaking the truth. Simplicity today, as in St. Vincent's time, means saying things as they are.

Truth is a keystone concept. It forms the basis of various philosophical and theological systems. For aristotelianism and scholastic philosophy, contemplation of the truth is the highest good. From a personalist perspective, truth is the foundation of trust, which is the basis of all human relations; falsehood, on the other hand, violates trust and makes genuine human relationships impossible.

Speaking and witnessing to the truth are central Christian values, especially in John's gospel. Jesus is the truth (4:6). The person who acts in the truth comes into the light (3:21). When the Spirit comes, he will guide us to all truth (16:13). It is the truth that sets us free (8:32). The reason why Jesus has come is to testify to the truth (18:37). Anyone who is of the truth hears his voice (18:37).

But experience proves that it is very difficult to let our *yes* mean *yes* and our *no* mean *no* (Mt 5:37; cf. Jas 5:12; 2 Cor 1:17-20), as Jesus puts it. It is precisely because Jesus speaks the truth that his enemies give him no credence (Jn 8:44). Ultimately, he dies for the truth.

---

1. Erik Erikson, *Gandhi's Truth* (New York, 1969).

On the other hand, as St. Vincent reminds us, there is a great attractiveness about those who speak the truth. We sense spontaneously that they have nothing to hide, that they have no hidden agendas. They are truly free. Consequently, it is easy to relate to them.

Yet speaking the truth with consistency is an extremely difficult discipline. We are tempted to blur the truth when our own convenience is at stake or when the truth is embarrassing to us personally. It is also difficult to be true to one's word, one's promises, one's commitments. When we make a statement in the present, it is either true or false right then and there. When we make a commitment for the future, however, it is true only to the extent that we keep it true. Truth, in this sense, is fidelity. It is in this sense especially that Jesus is true to us. He promises to be, and is, with us always, even to the end. It is in this same sense that we are called to be true to vows, to friendships, to our concrete commitments to serve.

Speaking the truth is especially important in the relationship we call "spiritual direction." We choose a "soul friend" so that, with his or her help, we might grow in the Lord's life and in discerning those things which promote his kingdom. It is imperative, therefore, that this relationship be characterized by free self-disclosure and by the avoidance of "hidden corners" in our lives. No one is an island. We need others to mirror back to us what is happening or not happening in our journey toward the Lord (cf. the second horizon-shift above). The quality of such relationships in spiritual direction will depend largely upon the simplicity with which we disclose ourselves.

b. Witnessing to the truth. This understanding of simplicity is most relevant. People spontaneously admire those who live out what they believe and say. A very comprehensive survey by the Association of Theological Schools[1] in the United States and Canada disclosed that the quality people most sought in ministers was genuineness, authenticity. This seems to be a perennial desire. The reader will recall Chaucer's praise of the parson in the *Canterbury Tales*:[2]

> *This noble example to his sheep he gave*
> *That first he wrought and afterward he taught.*

In an era when so many young people have lost confidence in civil and religious authorities because of corruption and proved duplicity (e.g., Water-

---

1. *Readiness for Ministry*, published by the Association of Theological Schools in the U.S. and Canada (Vandalia, Ohio) 1975-76.
2. *Canterbury Tales*, prologue, description of the parson.

gate and Irangate in the USA, the disclosures about the lives and life-styles of the Marcos family in the Philippines and of the Ceausescu family in Rumania), those whose lives match their words speak more powerfully than ever.

This type of simplicity is also extremely attractive in the modern world. Young people love those who are "real," "genuine." These are contemporary names for simplicity.

Such genuineness comes across to others as personal integrity, or a transparency that discloses inner richness. It assures others that they can believe in us. As Shakespeare put it:[1]

> *This above all: to thine own self be true*
> *And it must follow, as the night the day,*
> *Thou canst not then be false to any man.*

c. Seeking the truth. Being "real" or genuine today, as is evident from the first horizon-shift described above, may often demand our admission that we are groping to find the truth, that we are uncertain as to the truth, or that there are complementary truths. This is all the more necessary in a world where it is not longer possible to have universal knowledge.

We are conscious today of being wayfarers. Life is a journey, an ongoing process. So it is also with the quest for truth. We grasp the truth gradually. It is not captured in a single insight. Our verbal attempts at expressing it are always limited, perfectible. Nor is it possessed once for all. It is constructed bit by bit. The deeper we descend into the well, the deeper we know the well to be. So we must be dedicated to seeking, pursuing, finding the truth. This virtue, which Bernard Häring calls "dedication to the truth," takes the form of listening well, meeting and discussing with others, reading, ongoing education.

d. Being in the truth. This is what we might traditionally call simplicity of intention, purity of heart, referring all things to God. It is single-minded devotion to the Lord and his kingdom. In this sense, when the simple person labors, he labors because he loves God and he loves his people. He does not labor in order to be placed in high positions. Nor does he labor because admiration or money may come his way if he takes on extra work. When a simple person recognizes that his motives are mixed, he talks them out and seeks the aid of another to help him discern why he is really doing things. He knows that it is impossible always to have a single intention, but he seeks to make love of God and service of the neighbor the dominant motive in everything. If, as mentioned above in describing the fourth horizon-shift,

---

1. *Hamlet*, Act I, Scene 3.

Jesus groped to know his Father's will and struggled with contrary desires as he resolved to do it, the simple person today will necessarily engage in and work through a similar struggle.

As an aid in growing in this type of simplicity it is helpful to survey the competing values in our lives from time to time. Comfort, power, popularity, and financial security can subtly compete with love of God and love of neighbor. Sometimes these secondary motives will coincide with purer motives (as when the people whom we serve admire us and give us lots of positive feedback). But when they conflict, are we willing to sacrifice?

e. Practicing the truth (in love). This means performing works of justice and charity, making the truth come alive creatively in the world. It means bringing the truth to completion in deed. It means making our word become flesh, giving the gospels concrete life-form. The truth cannot just be verbal; it must be lived. Commitments to do the works of justice cannot just be spoken; they must be kept, day in and day out. The gospels cannot just be preached; they must be practiced in love.

Simplicity, from this point of view, means that when we preach justice we must also live justice. When we preach solidarity with the poor, we must also live in solidarity with the poor. When we exhort others to a simple life-style, we must live simply ourselves. When we say that we are celibate, we must live as celibates. When we proclaim the ways of peace-making, we must act as peace-makers.

f. Integration. Simplicity in this sense means personal wholeness, the ability to bring together in a unified way the varied aspects of one's life: labor, prayer, community, solitude, leisure. Young people speak of "having it together." Formation literature today often stresses integration as the goal of the whole formation process.

Martin Buber tells a striking story that illustrates the importance of integration:

A hasid of the Rabbi of Lublin once fasted from one Sabbath to the next. On Friday afternoon he began to suffer such cruel thirst that he thought he would die. He saw a well, went up to it, and prepared to drink. But instantly he realized that because of one brief hour he had still to endure, he was about to destroy the work of the entire week. He did not drink and went away from the well. Then he was touched by a feeling of pride for having passed this difficult test. When he became aware of it, he said to himself, "Better I go and drink than let my heart fall prey to pride." He went back to the well, but just as he was going to bend down to draw water, he noticed that his thirst had disappeared. When the Sabbath had begun, he entered his teacher's house. "Patchwork!" the rabbi called to him, as he crossed the threshold.[1]

The truly simple person arrives at "being a united soul." His life is no longer "patchwork," but is "all of a piece." Love of God and love of neighbor come together in a single whole.

g. Simplicity of life. As in St. Vincent's time, simplicity today also has implications in regard to life-style. Some contemporary writers even prefer to use the terminology "simplicity of life" to "poverty" when speaking of the content of our vow. Regardless of the terminology, our commitment to community for the service of the poor necessarily involves a commitment to a simple life-style, in which we share, at least in some ways, in the experience of those in need. More will be said about this when speaking of mortification (and in a later chapter, when speaking of the vow of poverty).

But such simplicity of life must not be confused, as sometimes happens, with drabness or lack of beauty (or worse, with lack of cleanliness!). On the contrary, simplicity implies beauty and enhances it. Simplicity is one of the characteristics of genuine art. Masterpieces of painting, sculpture, design, and music, even when quite complex, maintain a radical simplicity that lies at the heart of their beauty. Consequently, it is important to foster a sense of "the beautiful" in our lives. Especially the places and the forms of our prayer (singing, methods of reciting the psalms, images, etc.), while simple, should be "something beautiful for God."

2. Humility

It is difficult for modern men and women to accept St. Vincent's language when he speaks about humility. We tend to cringe when he calls himself the worst of all sinners and speaks of his community as the most wretched in the world.

Yet when he emphasizes humility, prescinding from the language in which he speaks, St. Vincent penetrates a basic abiding New Testament truth. St. Luke's gospel, in particular, tells us that God comes to the lowly, the poor of Israel, those who recognize their need from him and long for him. In this sense, humility is *the foundation of all evangelical perfection, the node of the whole spiritual life*" (CR II, 7). In this sense too, St. Vincent went to the core of the gospels when he said that *"humility is the origin of all the good that we do"* (IX, 674).

---

1. Martin Buber, "Resolution," in *The Way of Man According to the Teaching of the Hasidism* (Secaucus, N.J., 1966) 21.

Moving beyond St. Vincent's language and a rhetoric that was characteristic of the seventeenth century, it is important to articulate an understanding of humility and the contemporary forms that it takes.

a. Humility is a recognition of our creatureliness and our redeemedness, both being gifts of God's love.

We are completely dependent upon the Lord. "*In him we live and move and have our being*" (Acts 17:28).

There is nothing that we have not received. "*Truly you have formed my inmost being; you knit me in my mother's womb*" (Ps 139:13). Whatever we are, whatever we do, whatever we possess comes from the Lord.

We are also very much dependent on others. As mentioned in describing the second horizon-shift, the modern age is increasingly conscious of the interdependence of all men and women. The humble person recognizes interdependence both as a sign of his limitedness and as a source of enrichment. We need others and cannot do without them. In solidarity with them, we journey toward the kingdom.

Besides being creatures, we are sinners who have been redeemed through God's gracious love. "*All have sinned and are deprived of the glory of God. All are now undeservedly justified by the gift of God, through the redemption wrought in Christ Jesus*" (Rom 3:23-24).

Perhaps as a distorted reaction to an overemphasis on sin in the past, the modern age has difficulty sustaining a sense of sin (cf. the fifth horizon-shift described above). Yet sin, if we are alert to it, shows itself in numerous different ways in our lives: in our prejudices, in our tendency to categorize other people indiscriminately, in our speaking lightly about others' negative points, in our slowness to pray, in our inability to get excited about gospel values, in our selectivity in reading the gospels, in our unwillingness to share what we have with the poor, in our hesitancy to divest ourselves of power and to stand with the needy in their misery, in our compliance with unjust social structures. In face of all this, the Lord forgives us eagerly and gives us life in Christ Jesus. It is not by the works we do that we are saved, but rather by the gift of God in Christ Jesus (cf. Gal 2:21-22). Otherwise grace is not grace (Rom 11:6).

b. Humility is gratitude for gifts. In the New Testament, gratitude is the opposite side of the coin from humility. The person who has received all stands before the Lord in a spirit of thanksgiving. In this sense, thanksgiving is the central Christian attitude, which we celebrate as "eucharist" daily.

Mary epitomizes this attitude in Luke's gospel:

My being proclaims the greatness of the Lord.
My spirit finds joy in God my Savior for he has looked upon his
servant in her lowliness.

All ages to come shall call me blessed. God who is mighty has done great things for me.

Holy is his name. His mercy is from age to age on those who fear him. (Lk 1:46-50)

Mary cries out in praise and thanksgiving for the many gifts that God has given her. She recognizes God's gifts, without diminishing or denying them, and responds with gratitude. In this she echoes the psalmist: "Give thanks to the Lord for he is good for his loving kindness endures forever. Give thanks to the God of gods for his loving kindness endures forever" (Ps 136:1-3).

This type of gratitude characterizes the poor. Henri Nouwen writes:

> *Many poor people live in such close relationship with the many rhythms of nature that all the goods that come to them are experienced as free gifts of God. Children and friends, bread and wine, music and pictures, trees and flowers, water and life, a house, a room with just one bed, all are gifts to be grateful for and celebrated. This basic sense I have come to know. I am always surrounded by words of thanks, "Thanks for your visit, your blessing, your sermon, your prayer, your gifts, your presence with us." Even the smallest and most necessary goods are a reason for gratitude. This all-pervading gratitude is the basis for celebration. The poor not only are grateful for life, they also celebrate life constantly.*[1]

Recognizing that all is gift, the humble person will be eager to avoid comparisons. He or she will receive life with gratitude, leaving judgment to the Lord, as the gospels frequently exhort us to (cf. Mt 7:1-5). Pride loves comparison. The avaricious person may be satisfied when he possesses much; the proud person remains restless as long as anyone else has more. Humility spurns comparison. It can focus on the good in others, just as in oneself, and thank the Lord for it.

c. Humility involves a servant's attitude. This is central in the New Testament, especially for those who exercise authority. "*If anyone wishes to be first, he must be the last of all and the servant of all*" (Mk 9:35). In John's gospel Jesus demonstrates this for his disciples through a parable in action when he washes their feet.

> *Do you understand what I just did for you? You address me as "teacher" and "Lord," and fittingly enough for that is what I am. But if I washed your feet—I your teacher and Lord—then you must wash each other's feet. What I just did was to give you an example: as I have done so you must do.* (Jn 13:12-15)

---

1. Henri Nouwen "Humility" *America* (December 11, 1982) 372; cf. H. Nouwen *Gracias* (San Francisco, 1983) 146-47.

We are called, like Jesus, "not to be served but to serve" (Mt 20:28). This is especially imperative in light of the third horizon-shift described above. The expectation of the Church in the modern world is that authority figures will be collegial, dialogic, humble servants. An ancient Christian baptismal hymn captures this insight into Jesus and applies it to his followers:

> *Your attitude must be that of Christ. Though he was in the form of God he did not deem equality with God something to be grasped at. Rather he emptied himself and took the form of a slave, being born in the likeness of men. He was known to be of human estate, and it was thus that he humbled himself, obediently accepting even death, death on a cross. Because of this God highly exalted him and bestowed on him the name above every other name, so that at Jesus' name every knee must bend in the heavens, on the earth, and under the earth, and every tongue proclaim to the glory of God the Father: Jesus Christ is Lord!* (Phil 2:5-11)

As servants, we must be willing to do humble things. With the changed paradigm for the exercise of authority (cf. the third horizon-shift described above), leadership tasks that were once prestigious, like administration, may today truly be humble tasks, exposing the servant-leader to much criticism while engaging him in many meetings and humdrum paper work that brings little positive feedback.

d. Today, humility also entails allowing ourselves to be evangelized by the poor ("*our lords and masters*" as St. Vincent liked to call them). This insight, already present in the early Church and echoed later by St. Vincent, receives great emphasis in Latin American theology and in an ecclesiology "from below" (cf. the fourth horizon-shift described above).

Not only do we as ministers teach others, we must allow them to teach us. As St. Augustine put it, there are seeds of the Word everywhere and in everyone.[1] Only the humble can discern them. We must hear God speaking to us as we see the willingness of the poor to share the little that they have, as we see their gratitude to God for the simple gifts that he gives them, as we see their hoping against hope that God will provide, as we see their reverence and care and respect for us as well as for God. The poor will preach to us eloquently if we allow them.

3. Meekness

St. Vincent's teaching about this smooth stone is perhaps the most easily

---

1. Cf. *Evangelii Nuntiandi* 53.

translatable into modern usage. His conference of March 28, 1659, as well as several of his letters to Louise de Marillac, contain a practical wisdom that is very relevant today.

a. Meekness entails the ability to handle anger positively.

Anger is natural. It is energy that spontaneously arises within us when we perceive something as evil. It helps us to deal with evil but, like all spontaneous emotions, it can be used well or badly. Concretely, all sorts of people have trouble handling it well. There are many "angry people" in the world as a whole as well as in religious communities.

As St. Vincent pointed out, handling anger well often involves expressing it. He himself was outraged at the plight of the sick and the hungry, so he established the Confraternities of Charity, the Ladies of Charity, the Vincentians, and the Daughters of Charity. Anger enabled him to react with vigor and creativity when confronted with the needs of the poor in his day. He also expressed anger directly when he perceived evil within his communities, but he learned to combine his anger with gentleness. He knew how to mix the bitter and the sweet, as he told Louise de Marillac (I, 292-94). He sought to imitate Jesus who was equally "gentle and firm" (VII, 226). The witness of Jesus in this regard is all the more evident today in light of a Christology "from below" (cf. the fourth horizon-shift above).

But if anger is handled badly, it can be terribly destructive. Unleashed, it can result in violence and injustice. Repressed, it can result in resentment, sarcasm, cynicism, bitterness, depression.

Anger must at times be controlled, moderated, even suppressed for a period of time, or sublimated. St. Vincent again often appeals to the example of Jesus who knew how to moderate his frustration in regard to the apostles but who could be very direct in expressing his anger in regard to the Pharisees who were laying unjust burdens upon others.

b. Meekness entails approachability, gentleness. These are especially important qualities in ministers. In this regard, St. Vincent encourages us to know that we can really change. He tells us that when he was young he was of choleric temperament, easily angered. He says that he was very moody for long dark periods. But he changed so much in the course of his life that all those who knew him later said that he was one of the most approachable men they had ever met.

He told the community that people are won over much more by gentleness than by argument. This advice is especially relevant when we offer the gift of correction (cf. Mt 18:15-18), whether the correction is done by peers or by superiors. Those corrected are much more able to hear works spoken gently than words of stinging accusation.

c. Meekness involves the ability to endure offenses with forgiveness and courage. St. Vincent based his teaching in this regard on respect for the human person. Even those who commit injustice, he told the double family, deserve respect as persons. The writings of John Paul II reiterate this theme in our day.

Naturally, having respect for the person of the offender does not prohibit us from channeling our anger with courage against the evils the offender is committing. But it does prohibit us from practicing injustice in the name of justice. St. Vincent also recognized clearly (and he reminded Philip Le-Vacher about St. Augustine's teaching in this regard) that there are some evils that must be tolerated, since there is no practical possibility of correcting them. The wise man learns to live with them, and the meek man treats gently those whose lives are so entwined in them that the evil cannot be rooted out.

There is a delicate balance in this regard. At times one must suffer with courage. There are evils that cannot be avoided and that must be endured. On the other hand, one must avoid a false gentility, as Adrian Van Kaam puts it. At times one must cry out against injustice and channel all one's energies into overcoming it. It takes great prudence to know the difference between the two cases.

In this time of transition in the history of the Church (cf. especially the first and sixth horizon-shifts described above), the combination of gentleness and firmness is especially necessary. This is particularly so in making decisions. As communities assess their apostolates with a view toward the future, they must have the courage to choose and act. At the same time, they must show gentleness toward those who have difficulty adapting. Likewise, individuals must have courage in setting growth-goals, but they must be gentle with themselves in recognizing that personal change does not occur overnight, but only gradually.

Ministers too must know that no matter how well they do their jobs, they will have to endure, with both courage and gentleness, their own limitations and the conflicting expectations of others. Religious superiors will experience that some in their communities see all things in black and white, while others love only what is grey. Some will use the past as their norm for decision-making, while others will look only to an uncharted future. Superiors will never fully satisfy all, or even any, of these different personalities. They must make decisions with courage and treat with gentleness those who disagree. They must combine in their lives two New Testament sayings: "With the strength that comes from God, bear your share of the hardships the gospel entails" (2 Tm 1:8), and "Learn of me that I am meek and humble of heart and you will find rest for your souls" (Mt 11:29).

4. Mortification

It is unpopular to talk about mortification today.[1] It is becoming what Karl Rahner calls a "forgotten truth." Naturally, people shrink away from anything that connotes dying. Moreover, changes in perspective since the time of St. Vincent (cf. especially the fifth horizon-shift described above) have made some of the practices that he recommends seem irrelevant, even bizarre. These same changes have made young people question even the theoretical underpinnings of the traditional teaching about mortification. They question the clean-cut division of the human person into animal and rational, with sin dominating the animal side (and not the rational side?). They ask: why not stop to smell the flower along the roadside? Why not gaze at the beauty of God in creation? Why not think back in gratitude on the love our parents gave us?

At the same time, interestingly, some of the most popular modern writers recommend discipline, a form of mortification, strongly. Gandhi says that nothing is accomplished without discipline and prayer.[2] Erich Fromm says that discipline is the first step in the practice of loving.[3] Dietrich Bonhoeffer describes discipline as one of the stations on the way to freedom.[4]

In retrieving the value involved in mortification, it seems best to admit frankly that a change in theological perspective (cf. especially the third, fifth, and sixth horizon-shifts above) has made some of the practices St. Vincent recommended irrelevant today and some of the theoretic involved in his teaching outdated and one-sided. St. Vincent had a much more negative attitude toward created reality than we would have. When he recommends bypassing the flower on the roadside as a way of mortifying ourselves, modern men and women rightly ask why they should not pick it up, smell it, enjoy its beauty and praise God as its creator.

Still, St. Vincent grasped how important mortification is. Along with all of the saints, he believed the Lord when he told them that, to be his follower, they must deny themselves. I offer the following perspective as an attempt at retrieving the value of mortification in the modern world.

a. Mortification involves renouncing one good thing in order to do a better thing.

In this sense, it is "functional asceticism," to use Karl Rahner's phrase.[5]

---

1. Margaret Myles states: "Asceticism is one of the currently least understood and most universally rejected features of historical Christianity." Cf. *Practicing Christianity. Critical Perspectives for an Embodied Spirituality* (New York, 1988) 94.
2. Thomas Merton (ed.), *Gandhi on Non-Violence* (New York, 1965) 24ff.
3. Erich Fromm, *Art of Loving* (New York, 1956) 108.
4. D. Bonhoeffer, *Ethics* (New York, 1955) 15.
5. Karl Rahner, *Theological Investigations* VIII, 208.

Mortification is always for the sake of something or someone else. It is "for my sake and for the gospels." We give up good things not because we think they are bad. We acknowledge that they are good even as we give them up, because we want something better. A person may decide to cut out smoking because he wants to be in good health, or to cut down on or abstain from drinking because he wants to be clear-headed and self-possessed in thinking, judging and acting. A person may embrace celibacy in order to be "free for the Lord" or in order to dedicate himself or herself single-mindedly to the service of the kingdom wherever the Lord asks them to go, or in order to give themselves over to a life of prayer. A person may renounce material possessions because he wants to share them with the poor or because he wants to enter into solidarity with the poor by sharing their lot. A person may renounce his freedom to choose whatever he wants to do because he chooses to live in community and to join with others in a common life and common project. In this sense, the real purpose of mortification is to choose and to construct one's real self.[1]

b. Mortification involves recognizing our goals and channeling our limited energies into achieving them.

We cannot do everything in life. We are really very limited. It is the rare person who can be a great piano player, or a superstar in basketball, or a wonderful actor. No one combines all of these things. They all take time, practice, disciplined labor. The time needed to become a great piano player works against the time needed to become a basketball superstar or a great doctor.

Consequently, it is imperative that a person know what his goals are and that he give himself in a disciplined way to accomplishing them. That is why Jesus says that no one can be his follower unless he renounces house, wife, father, mother, brother, sister, all things for my sake and for the gospel. If our first goal is to follow Jesus, then our attachment to everything else must be modified in light of that goal.

c. Mortification is also "practicing for death," to use another of Karl Rahner's phrases.[2]

We experience death as darkness. It is the ultimate renunciation. It demands that we let go of life, our most basic possession. The limitedness that we experience as creatures challenges us again and again to let go of one thing in order that we might pursue another more single-mindedly. Only the

---

1. Cf. Myles, *op. cit.*, 96-97: "The *same* energy that originally organized the person's pursuit of sex, power, and possessions can be removed from the socially conditioned self and relocated in the religious self. . . . The real point of ascetic practices, then, was not to 'give up' objects, but to reconstruct the self."
2. Karl Rahner, *Theological Investigations* III, 54.

person who is practiced in this art will be able to hand himself over to his Father in an act of final resignation, as Jesus did: "Father, into your hands I commend my spirit" (Lk 23:46). A Christology "from below" (cf. the fourth horizon-shift above) emphasizes the struggle that Jesus experienced in his dying and calls us to enter into it with him.

d. In light of what has been said above, let me mention some contemporary forms that mortification might take. The list is by no means exhaustive; on the contrary, the author hopes that the reader will find in it a stimulus for thinking about other forms.

1. Being ready to respond to the needs of one's religious community and God's people, particularly in accepting assignments. The calls of God's people are very important. Our own gifts and talents are too. Most modern religious communities attempt to fit calls to the gifts and talents of their individual members. In this context, it is imperative for us to let ourselves be challenged. Often, responses to challenges draw forth from us resources whose existence we are even unaware of.

2. Being faithful to the duties of one's state in life; preferring them when they conflict with other more pleasurable things. This is more difficult than may appear on first bounce. It is very important to know what the central values in our lives are: apostolate, prayer, community, study, etc. Experience teaches us that these often become less attractive than other options, especially in the long run and especially if the other options provide more immediate gratification. The modern era tends to despise delayed gratification. Options like watching TV passively or spending great amounts of time with comforting but unchallenging companions (what is commonly called today "protective partnership") can easily distract us from the central values in our lives.

3. Working hard as servants do. Much of the work that religious are engaged in is non-structured. Our time is our own to be used responsibly. To do this requires discipline. Much time can be frittered away.

4. Rising promptly in the morning to praise God and strengthen our brothers and/or sisters by joining them in prayer. St. Vincent felt strongly about this. He judged that without prayer (and prompt rising for it) his community could not continue to exist. It is important to pray in a disciplined way, to set time aside daily, and to support others in the endeavor.

5. Being sparing in obtaining or accepting material possessions, like clothing, or money, or other items; in other words, developing a simple life-style. This is what Karl Rahner calls "consumer asceticism." Such asceticism is very difficult in our society and very different from what

society propagandizes us to do. The contemporary world again and again in its advertisements tells us that it is always good to have more.

6. Being disciplined in eating and drinking, and avoiding all anxiety or complaint about what we shall eat or what we shall drink. The key here is moderation. It is good to avoid griping about food. St. Vincent felt strongly about this. He also recommended not eating between meals. This can still be a good ascetical practice as an aid in keeping one's weight down and staying in good physical condition.

7. Employing moderation and a critical sense in using television, radio, movies, and other media. There is much waste of time in the modern world. There is much passive entertainment. There is much uncritical drinking in of violence and sexual license. One of the consequences of this is that the lives of many people tend to become like those of characters whom they watch on the soap operas. What we take in through the senses, especially if it is a steady diet, inevitably influences our conduct bit by bit.

8. Being slow to ask for privileges or to be the exception from what is the norm. Norms are for the common good. In contemporary religious communities they are usually made after much consultation. They are also usually few in number. It is helpful to the common well-being if we allow ourselves to be supportive of the few norms that we do have.

9. Withholding critical and divisive words. This can be a great aid to charity. St. Benedict said that murmuring was the greatest vice of monasteries. St. Vincent felt similarly. It is a healthy norm to withhold critical words unless we can speak them constructively to those who can do something about them.

10. Seeking equally to be with those who are less pleasing to us as with those to whom we are more attracted. This is a great aid to life in common. We are brothers and sisters in the Lord. Naturally, we will always be closer to some people than to others. It is important to have good, intimate friends. Still, it is likewise important not to exclude others from our company and to have open-ended friendships that allow others to enter in.

11. Giving generously of our time in order to take part in contemporary decision-making processes (e.g., meetings, questionnaires, letters of consultation). This is very much a part of modern asceticism. It is, as some say, the "contemporary hair shirt." Part of obedience today is to participate (cf. the third horizon-shift described above). This is not simply a luxury. Nor is it the privilege of a few. All are called to take part in decision-making and responsible obedience. We are asked to

express our views openly. This is time-consuming and sometimes painful. As such, it is a mortification for most.

5. Zeal for souls[1]

Because the modern age emphasizes promotion of the whole person and tends to avoid the body/soul dichotomy, St. Vincent's phrase "zeal for souls" rings badly. Still, zeal is quite as important today as it was in St. Vincent's time. It has very much the same meaning.

a. Zeal is love on fire. It is a willingness to go anywhere, even under difficult circumstances, to speak of Christ. It is a willingness to die for him. It involves not only deep human *affective* love for the Lord and for his people, but it also expresses itself in *effective* labor and sacrifice.

As in the past, zeal expresses itself in our own day in martyrdom (in Central America, for example), but zealous people, now as always, also recognize that it is sometimes harder to live for Christ than to die for him. Their zeal shows itself in a willingness to continue to labor in the inner city in the face of the discouragement that flows from dire poverty and from tangling with bureaucracy. It shows itself in the life and work of missionaries who struggle with language, culture, food, climate.

b. Zeal is persevering, faithful love. It is easy to love for a time. It is difficult to love for life. Permanent commitment is more fragile today than it was in the seventeenth century, especially since many of the societal supports that undergirded it at that time have disappeared (cf. the fifth and sixth horizon-shifts described above). So zeal shows itself today especially as fidelity. It is gold tested in the fire. It is creative in finding ways of loving both "in season and out of season." As St. Vincent put it, "Love is inventive, even to infinity" (XI, 146). Zeal adjusts, finding new ways and developing professionally, especially through ongoing formation. In this era of second careers and early retirement, it seeks to find ways of expressing love for the Lord and love for the poor even in ministries that may be quite different from the ways in which one served in his or her youth. This challenge which zeal presents today was not unknown to St. Vincent: "As for myself, in spite of my age, I say before God that I do not feel exempt from the obligation of laboring for the salvation of those poor people, for what could hinder me from doing so? If I cannot preach every day, all right! I will preach twice a

---

1. Cf. Jean-François Gaziello, "Les vertus du service," in *Monsieur Vincent, Témoin de L'Evangile* (Toulouse, 1990) 187-198, cf. also Christian Sens, "Comme Prêtre Missionaire" 149-151; J.-P. Renouard, "La gloire de Dieu et le règne de Jésus-Christ" 96-98.

week. If I cannot preach more important sermons, I will strive to preach less important ones; and if the people do not hear me, then what is there to prevent me from speaking in a friendly, homely way to those poor folk, as I am now speaking to you, gathering them around me as your are now?" (XI, 136).

c. Zeal shows itself in a willingness to seek laborers for the harvest. Love is infectious. Fire spreads. A love that is on fire will seek to communicate itself to others. It will seek to draw others into the same wonderful mission that it is carrying out.

A contemporary survey[1] notes that the most significant single factor in hindering young people from entering religious life is lack of encouragement from religious themselves and from one's family. One need hardly point out that there is a critical shortage of laborers for the harvest in many parts of the world today. The Church needs ministers. Zeal should impel us to encourage others to follow the Lord in various ministries. It should move us to speak to them directly and ask them if they have considered priesthood or brotherhood or sisterhood. Jesus did not hesitate to call the apostles directly. Nor should we, especially in an era when contemporary advertising bombards young people with numerous other calls and numerous other stimuli. If we really love what we are doing, then zeal will move us to involve others in doing it too.

d. The two extremes which St. Vincent contrasts with zeal also have contemporary forms that it may be helpful to say a word about.

1) The existentialists note that the great problem of modern men and women is inattentiveness. We live in a world filled with noise. So many sounds and stimuli break in upon us that at times it is difficult to distinguish the more important ones from the less important. As a result people's sensitivities can be dulled. They can be blind to the glaring problems that exist, especially the ever-increasing disparity between the rich and the poor and the continuing expenditure of human and financial resources in the production and sales of arms (cf. the second horizon-shift above). "Inattentiveness" can be the modern form of what St. Vincent described as "laxity, lack of fervor and sensitivity, sloth."

2) Indiscreet zeal likewise still shows itself in overwork and in what is often called "burn-out." It is quite as important today, as it was in St. Vincent's day,[2] that we know our limitations, accept our creatureli-

---

1. Cf. *Origins*, vol. 13 #39 (March 8, 1984), 652ff.
2. A Jesuit, who was working with the confreres, wrote to St. Vincent upon the death of Germain de Montevit: "Your men are flexible and docile about everything, except the advice they are given to take a little bit of rest. They believe that their bodies are not made of flesh, or that their life is supposed to last only a year" (SV II, 24).

ness, and develop a balanced life-style that includes sufficient rest and recreation. It is also important that we stay in good physical condition so that we will have the energy which characterizes zeal.

One final word. The word *character* usually denotes a seal, a sign, a visible mark by which someone or something can be recognized. The virtues described above in seventeenth and twentieth century forms are, to use St. Vincent's phrase, the *characteristic* virtues of his followers. They are the signs by which his followers are meant to be recognized. It is vitally important that each era reinterpret these signs in order that the spirit of St. Vincent might continue to live in a way that is relevant in each succeeding age. The author offers the preceding thoughts as a small contribution toward that end and welcomes the comments of others who might wish to advance the endeavor further.

Chapter III

THE FOUR VINCENTIAN VOWS:
YESTERDAY AND TODAY

Those who become detached from the desire for worldly goods, from the longing for pleasure, and from their own will become children of God. They enjoy perfect freedom. For it is only in the love of God that real freedom is found. They are people who are free, who know no law, who fly, who go left and right, who fly still more. No one can hold them back. They are never slaves of the devil nor of their own passions. Oh, how happy is the freedom of the children of God!

SV XII, 301

Since the publication of the previous chapter in an earlier form,[1] many people have encouraged me to attempt something similar in regard to the four Vincentian vows.[2] I am grateful for their stimulating me to engage in the research and reflection whose fruits I offer below. As with all such projects, I have been helped enormously by the research of others,[3] particularly in the first part of the chapter. But I have also attempted to examine the writings of St. Vincent anew.

1. "Five Characteristic Virtues: Yesterday and Today," *Vincentiana* 29 (1985) 226-254.
2. Many have encouraged me by their use of my article on the five virtues in retreats and formation programs and by their translating it into various languages. But I am especially grateful to J.-O. Baylach, former editor of *Vincentiana*, who was the first to suggest the idea of another article focusing on the vows. I hope that what I have written here addresses the topic at least somewhat adequately.
3. I wish to express my gratitude to the committee which prepared the "Program for Vincentian Formation in the Major Seminary of the Congregation of the Mission." We spent many hours together reflecting on the vows. Likewise, I thank the Superior General and the members of the General Council. On numerous occasions we have shared with one another and written our reflections on evangelical poverty as lived in the Congregation. Of course, I am also indebted to many others who have written at length on the vows, many of whom will be cited in the course of this article.

In that sense, for better or for worse, I stand responsible before the reader for the final outcome. Let me say from the start that I recognize the limitations of what I have written, particularly in the third part of the chapter. I invite reactions and criticism. In a climate of dialogue, or what John Courtney Murray liked to call "civilized argument,"[1] we will, I would hope, grow in understanding and deepening our commitment to the vowed life.

In this chapter I will not attempt to narrate the interesting history of St. Vincent's efforts to have the vows of the Congregation approved by the Holy See. Others have treated this topic exhaustively.[2] Nor will I be examining, except in passing, the juridical status of our vows, a topic frequently treated elsewhere.[3] My objective is to focus on the *meaning* of the Vincentian vows yesterday and today. In pursuing that end, I will not try to paint a complete picture of the historical backdrop for living the vows in the seventeenth century. This has been done exceedingly well by several others.[4] I will, however, make frequent allusion to those historical circumstances. Without such reference, one could not really interpret the concrete meaning of the vows.

To be even more specific, the direct focus of this chapter is on the meaning of the four vows pronounced, in St. Vincent's time and ours, by priests, deacons, brothers, and seminarians of the Congregation of the Mission. But, beyond this immediate audience, I do hope that many of the thoughts

---

1. John Courtney Murray, *We Hold These Truths* (N.Y.: Sheed and Ward, 1960) 14.
2. Cf. the very interesting treatment of this subject in J-M. Román, *San Vicente de Paul* (Madrid: BAC, 1981) 322-44; P. Coste, *The Life and Works of St. Vincent de Paul,* trans. by J. Leonard (New York: New City Press, 1978) I, 479-498; also L. Mezzadri, *San Vincenzo de Paul* (Turin: Edizioni Paoline, 1986) 148-150.
3. Cf. H. De Graaf, *De Votis quae Emittuntur in Congregatione Missionis* (Nijmegen, 1955); CPAG-1980, "The Congregation of the Mission: Its Vows and the Bond between Members and Community," published in mimeographed form in preparation for the General Assembly of 1980; "Declaration of the 36th General Assembly of the Congregation of the Mission concerning the Identity of the Same Congregation," *Vincentiana* 24 (1980), 256; cf. also Const. 55. Cf. also *Brevia et Decreta Considerate Legenda Ante Emissionem Votorum* (Lutetiae Parisiorum, 1882); *Explications Sommaires des Règles Communes de la Congrégation de la Mission* (Paris, 1901); *Explanatio Votorum Quae Emittuntur in Congregatione Missionis* (Parisiis, 1909; 1911); J. Fernández Martínez, *Extensión del Voto de Pobreza en la Congregación de la Misión* (Madrid, 1940); Jacobus Brufau Maciá, *De Egressu e Congregatione Missionis* (Tegucigalpa, 1959).
4. For a brief summary and a basic bibliography, cf. R. Deville, *L'école française de spiritualité* (Paris: Desclée, 1987) 15-27. Cf. also Louis Cognet, "Ecclesiastical Life in France," in *History of the Church 6: The Church in the Age of Absolutism and Enlightenment,* ed. Hubert Jedin and John Dolan, trans. Gunther Holst (New York; Crossroad, 1981) 3-106; Victor-L. Tapié, *France in the Age of Louis XIII and Richelieu,* tr. and ed. by D. McN. Lockie (London: Macmillan, 1974); *Bérulle and the French School, Selected Writings,* edited with an introduction by William Thompson (New York: Paulist Press, 1989); *Christian Spirituality, Post-Reformation and Modern,* edited by Louis Dupré and Don Saliers (New York: Crossroad, 1989).

presented, both theoretical and practical, will also be useful, at least in part, to the Daughters of Charity and to the huge number of lay men and women who look to St. Vincent de Paul for their inspiration.

I have written the text in such a way that it can be read in its entirety without the numerous footnotes. But for those who wish to study the text at greater length (in houses of formation, for example), I have attempted to offer abundant references, some of which may be of considerable interest.

The chapter is divided into three parts: 1) the four vows as described by St. Vincent; 2) horizon-shifts that have taken place between the seventeenth and the twentieth century; 3) the four vows today.

PART I - THE FOUR VOWS AS DESCRIBED BY ST VINCENT

As was the case with the founders of many communities, St. Vincent saw the vows as both an offensive and defensive "weapon":[1]

> *Our Lord came into the world to reestablish the reign of his Father in all persons. He won them back from the devil who had led them astray by the cunning deceit of a greedy desire for wealth, honor and pleasure. Our loving Savior thought it right to fight his enemy with the opposite weapons, poverty, chastity and obedience, which he continued to do right up to his death.*

In forging his "weapons," St. Vincent drew on the long historical tradition of the Church, particularly as he found it in the rule written by St. Ignatius for the Society of Jesus.[2] Naturally, he also added his own touches, adjusting his "arms" to the historical circumstances of seventeenth-century France and to the specific type of Congregation he wished to found. Concretely, he knew that the members of his Company would be living in a world where the temptation to riches, or the "easy" clerical life was very real; he himself had experienced, and given into, this temptation at an earlier stage in his life, seeking a comfortable benefice with which to support himself and his family. Likewise, he saw that in seventeenth-century France faithful celibate living would be no small challenge; while there were some striking role-models among the reforming bishops and clergy of the day, witness to celibacy on

---

1. *Common Rules* II, 18 (henceforth, CR). It is interesting to note that for historical reasons (particularly his desire to avoid having the members of the Congregation classified as religious) St. Vincent avoids the term vows in the Common Rules, though he gives a rather thorough description of their content. Cf. his statement in SV XII, 367: "No mention is made of these three vows in our rules, because no Company such as ours has ever mentioned them in its Common Rules."

2. Cf. Román, *Ibid.* 322.

the part of many others was dismal.[1] Authority too, both local and Roman, was on the defensive. The episcopacy was in urgent need of reform, with some bishops rarely residing in their dioceses.[2] Civil authorities, moreover, often interfered with what local bishops and Rome attempted to do. The general atmosphere in France, particularly during the Jansenist controversy, was filled with rumblings against ultramontane forces. Finally, and perhaps most important, St. Vincent experienced painfully that many who began good works among the poor failed to persevere in them. He felt the gnawing need, to use his analogy, for stable "armed forces."

It was in this context that on September 22, 1655, after much struggle, St. Vincent received papal approval[3] for the members of his Congregation to pronounce vows of poverty, chastity, obedience, and stability, while still remaining members of the secular clergy,[4] but exempt from the power of the local ordinary, except in matters pertaining to their mission.[5] Only the pope and the Superior General, when dismissing someone from the Congregation, could dispense from these vows. Vincent hoped that, through pronouncing such vows, his missionaries would renew and deepen the gift of themselves to God for the service of the poor[6] and that later, in time of trial, they would be strengthened by recalling that they had committed themselves for life to this service.[7]

In reflecting on the vows, as well as on other matters pertaining to the

---

1. Cf. P. Coste, *Ibid.* I, 243f.; Román, *Ibid.* 123; 191-93; also L. Mezzadri, *Ibid.* 53-54; M. Roche, *St. Vincent de Paul and the Formation of Clerics* (Fribourg: University Press, 1964), 1-7. Cf. also SV XI, 308-10.
2. A couplet published by Racine in 1682 (cf. Deville, *Ibid.*, 16) reads:
An order came from St. Germain yesterday.
They're calling for a meeting, a meeting tomorrow.
Our archbishop and 52 others,
Successors of the apostles,
Will attend. But to know what they'll treat
That's a mystery.
There's only one thing very clear:
That we have 52 prelates
Who don't live in their dioceses. (Trans. mine)
3. Alexander VII, *Ex commissa nobis*; cf. SV XIII, 380-82.
4. While St. Vincent did not want the members of the Congregation to have the kind of vows religious had, he was convinced that, apart from all juridical considerations, the vows pronounced in the Company had the same value as those of religious. Cf. SV XII, 375: "Though we do not make solemn vows, we receive the same or similar graces as those received by professed religious."
5. Alexander VII, *Ex commissa nobis*. Cf. Coste, XIII, 380-82.
6. Cf. also A. Dodin, "Los votos en la espiritualidad vicenciana," in *Vicente de Paúl, pervivencia de un fundador* (Salamanca, 1972) 110-11; Dodin highlights St. Vincent's use of the phrase "to give oneself to God," used so often by St. Vincent in the prayers with which he closed his conferences. Cf., e.g., SV IX, 26, 534, 592; X, 513; XII, 323; XII, 354. Cf. also J.-M. Román, *Ibid.* 341.
7. SV XI, 233.

Congregation, it is important to note that what St. Vincent said and wrote is only a part of what he actually taught.[1] His practice modified his theory.[2] Sometimes, in fact, what he did contrasted markedly with his written and spoken word. I will allude to these differences in the course of this chapter where they are relevant.

Below, I will present what St. Vincent, by his words, writings and actions, taught about the meaning of the vows. I will make no attempt to defend statements or practices which might seem strange to the modern reader, except occasionally to describe the historical context that made the teaching intelligible in its time. Just as any reader must make adjustments in reading Shakespeare, Descartes, Pascal, or Cervantes (all more or less contemporaries of St. Vincent), so must one make the effort to understand Vincent in his own situation and strive to find the real sense in what he taught, rather than dismiss it too quickly as antiquated. The third part of this chapter will attempt to retrieve the meaning of St. Vincent's teaching for today.

Let me also say, as a final preliminary remark (one that will be repeated frequently in examining each vow), that for understanding the Vincentian vows it is imperative to see them as being in the service of the mission. For St. Vincent, the vows are not merely a matter of personal piety. They are "arms" to equip the missionary to serve the poor zealously and perseveringly. Though Vincent did, like Jesus, speak to his followers about the personal merit ("treasure in heaven") that they would gain by living the vowed life, he saw the vows, on a much deeper level, as ways of following Christ more faithfully in the *mission* his Father had given him to preach good news to the poor.[3]

Keeping these preliminary remarks in mind, we may now formulate in concrete fashion, and then examine, the basic question which the first part of this chapter addresses: having known and heard St. Vincent, just what did the 130 priests, 44 clerics and 52 lay brothers who were members of the Congregation[4] on September 27, 1660, understand as they reflected on the vows of the Company?

---

1. Cf. Dodin, *op. cit.*, 11: "Es necesario, repite, tomando la expresión de san Francisco de Sales y de santa Juana de Chantal, ser invariable en el fin, pero flexible y cambiante en los medios. Esta maxima es el 'alma de la buena conducta.' " For some details about St. Vincent's flexibility, cf. T. Davitt, "Some Less-Publicised Facets of St. Vincent," *Colloque* V, 14-23.
2. Recognition of this fact is all the more important since today we have probably only a tenth of the letters that St. Vincent wrote and a very small fraction of the conferences that he gave to the Vincentians, the Daughters of Charity and the Visitation nuns. For a very interesting account of sources available at the time of Abelly, cf. A. Dodin, *La légende et l'histoire de Monsieur Depaul à saint Vincent de Paul* (Paris: OEIL, 1985) 84-101.
3. SV XII, 366, 372.
4. For these and other similar statistics, cf. A. Dodin, "San Vicente de Paúl, místico de la acción religiosa," in *Vicente de Paúl, pervivencia de un fundador* (Salamanca, 1972) 62-63.

1. Poverty

His teaching

St. Vincent sees a life of evangelical poverty as an utter necessity in a Congregation dedicated to the evangelization of the poor. Without it, the Congregation will cease to exist.[1] Poverty is our foundation stone.[2] Using the language of warfare once again, he calls it "an unbreachable rampart"[3] by which the Congregation will be preserved forever. To encourage the confreres to live it, he places before them the example of Jesus, his apostles, and the first Christians,[4] and reminds them that in Matthew's gospel Jesus makes it the first of the beatitudes and the condition for perfection.[5]

He urges the members to have a deep affective love for poverty and also to put it into effective practice. But there is a delicate balance to be maintained on the practical side. St. Vincent recognizes right from the start that, because of their work in the missions, they will not be able to live a life of strict poverty, like the mendicant orders.[6] Yet still, in that context, the things they necessarily have—like their food, their rooms, their beds—should be similar to those of a poor person. They should be willing to experience at least some of the sting of poverty.[7]

Basically, St. Vincent tells the priests and brothers, the use of all things is to be in common.[8] If they have funds or property, they can retain their ownership even after pronouncing vows. Likewise, they can be the heirs of their parents' property.[9] If they should leave the Company, this property is theirs. In their wills, they may deed it to anyone they wish. But, while members of the Company, they may not use it or any revenues coming from it without the permission of superiors, and, even then, it should be used in good works.[10]

---

1. SV XI, 223.
2. SV XI, 78.
3. CR III, 1; SV XI, 232..
4. CR III, 1,3; Cf. SV XI, 263: "The state of Missionaries is an apostolic state which consists, as did the state of the apostles, in leaving and abandoning all things to follow Jesus Christ, and to become true Christians." Cf. also SV XI, 224-25; XII, 367-68.
5. SV XI, 246; XII, 380; XII, 388; cf. Mt 5:3 and 19:21. St. Vincent also alludes to many other scripture passages; cf. SV XII, 388-89. On St. Vincent's use of scripture, cf. A. Dodin, "M. Vincent de Paul et la Bible," *Vincentiana* XXXIV, 86-101; Warren Dicharry, "Saint Vincent and Sacred Scripture," *Vincentian Heritage* X, 136-48.
6. CR III, 2.
7. CR III, 7.
8. SV XI, 223: "Although there are some who have possessions, they do not use them as if they were their own, though they retain radical dominion over them."
9. Cf. SV IV, 11-12, where St. Vincent explains this to Louis Thibault.
10. Alexander VII, *Alias nos supplicationibus*; cf. SV XIII, 406-409. Cf. also the conference of November 14, 1659 (SV XII, 383), in which St. Vincent outlines for the confreres the

St. Vincent sees clearly that the practice of poverty will liberate the confreres. They will be willing to go anywhere, to do anything, to brave all hardships, if they are attached to nothing.[1] Without this virtue, they will not persevere in the Company.[2] As was the case with Judas, avarice is the root of all evil.[3] But on the deepest level, if they are to be truly free, they must renounce not merely material things, but all other attachments.[4] In fact, they must renounce their very selves.[5] Their renunciation must not be just external; rather, it must come from the heart. True peace of mind will then follow.[6]

St. Vincent is concerned not just about individual poverty, but also about the poverty (and consequent liberty) of the Company. He writes to Jacques Chiroye, superior at Luçon, in 1650: "In the name of God, let us be more concerned about extending the kingdom of Jesus Christ than about our own possessions. If we take care of his affairs, he will take care of ours."[7]

He was convinced that, like all virtues, poverty could be acquired by repeated acts.[8] In the Common Rules, he lists a number of concrete practices which he judged would keep the spirit of poverty alive in the Company:[9]

- items like food, clothing, books, and furniture will be for common use and superiors will distribute them to each according to need;[10]
- no one will have any possessions without the knowledge of the superior and each shall be willing to give up such possessions at the superior's command;[11]
- confreres shall not use possessions as if they were their own;[12]
- nor shall they give things away, receive them, lend them out, or take them from one house to another without the permission of the superior;[13]
- they shall not neglect the goods they have or allow them to deteriorate;[14]

---

meaning of the fundamental statute on poverty.
1. SV XI, 228. Cf. also X, 513.
2. SV XI, 237.
3. SV XI, 242-43.
4. SV XI, 246.
5. SV XII, 381. For St. Vincent, this includes "judgment, will, inclinations, desires and passions."
6. SV XII, 370: "One of the advantages of this state is the peace of mind we enjoy, having, by our vows, renounced all things."
7. SV III, 531-32; cf. also VIII, 151-52.
8. SV XI, 247.
9. In this regard, it is also interesting to read the list of faults given by St. Vincent in the conferences of October 16 and 23, 1654; cf. SV XI, 163-64.
10. CR III, 3; SV XI, 246. In the conference of November 21, 1659, St. Vincent comments on the various practices stipulated in the Common Rules; cf. SV XII, 386f.
11. CR III, 4,6.
12. CR III, 5.
13. CR III, 3, 5, 6, 9.
14. CR III, 6.

- they shall not own superfluous items nor curiosities;[1]
- they shall avoid giving the impression of ownership; their rooms should not be locked, nor should they have anything locked with a private key, unless with the expressed permission of the superior.[2]

Since temptations against poverty can come in spiritual guise, the Rules forbid the confreres to desire benefices or ecclesiastical dignities, both of which could be sources of considerable enrichment.[3] If confreres got involved in that, the Congregation, St. Vincent felt, would become quickly destabilized, with members entering and leaving rapidly.

The missionary dimension of the vow of poverty is paramount for Vincent. He was convinced that if we become attached to material possessions, "then we can say goodbye to the works of the Mission, and even to the Mission itself, for it will no longer exist."[4] Providence is the real guarantee of our future, not material goods.[5]

Practice modifying theory

But, as was often the case with St. Vincent, practice modified theory. He was a man of great common sense and practical wisdom, which he applied to concrete cases that arose.

While he forcefully urged the members of the Company to live a simple life-style, at the same time he wanted superiors to be careful to supply the needs of the confreres. In a delightful letter, he tells Antoine Colée, superior at Toul: "I have heard that your bread was not well made. Please have it done by a baker, if you can find one, for the most important thing is to have good bread. It would also be well to vary the food sometimes . . . to relieve the strain on poor nature which tires of seeing the same things all the time."[6] In advising Antoine Durand, who had just been named superior at Agde, he urges him to be very attentive to temporal affairs, adding: "When the Son of God sent out his apostles, at first he recommended that they not bring any

---

1. CR III, 7.
2. CR III, 8. In speaking of the means for practicing poverty, St. Vincent suggests that superiors visit the rooms. With great simplicity, he states in a conference in 1654: "I ask the officers of the house to see to this. Let a beginning be made tomorrow with my room, then Fr. Portail's, then those of Fr. Almeras . . ." Cf. SV XI,164-65. Cf. also the conference of December 5, 1659 (SV XII, 408-409), where St. Vincent treats the problem of those rummaging around in the rooms of others.
3. CR III, 10. St. Vincent comments on this rule in a conference given on Nov. 28, 1659; cf. SV XII, 399-403.
4. SV XI, 79.
5. SV VIII, 151; cf. also IX, 56-57.
6. Cf. SV I, 387.

money. But later on, as the number of his disciples grew, he decided to have a bursar in the group, who was charged not just with feeding the poor, but also with tending to the needs of his family."[1]

Recognizing that rules and laws are to be applied to the general run of cases, not to every particular one, he was willing to make reasonable exceptions, especially when the end of the law could be preserved. Though in the Rule he forbids accepting benefices, he was on occasion not loath to accept them, as well as other sources of revenue, sometimes even burdensome ones, if it was a question of getting the funds to establish a mission on a firm foundation.[2]

His concern for the material well-being of the Company was so great that it even moved him to go against the evangelical maxims. "I have great pain, for reasons you can imagine, in going against the advice of Our Lord, who did not want his followers to take legal action" he writes to Monsieur Desbordes, a counsellor in Parliament,[3] "and if we have already done it, it is because I could not in conscience give up something so legitimately acquired, community property of which I have charge. . . ."

2. Chastity

His teaching

In seeking to understand what St. Vincent says about chastity, it is important to note the thought patterns of the era in which he lived. The view of human sexuality expressed in the spiritual reading books and theological literature available to St. Vincent in early seventeenth-century France was largely negative[4]. The arrival of Jansenism, with its moral rigorism and its

---

1. SV XI, 350.
2. Cf. J.-M. Román, "The Foundations of St. Vincent," *Vincentian Heritage* 9 (1988), 153-59.
3. SV VII, 406-407.
4. At the end of his chapters on chastity, Alphonsus Rodriguez, whose famous book, *Practice of Perfection and Christian Virtues,* was being read at table at St. Lazare on May 17, 1658 (cf. SV XII, 12) tells an anecdote which is illustrative of the attitude of contemporary spiritual writers: "Father Master Avila quotes an instance of a holy hermit to whom God had granted to know the great danger to which he lay exposed in this life; and, considering that, he put over his head a hood of mourning and covered his face in such manner that he could see nothing but the ground he was to tread upon, and never more would speak to man, and never more took his eyes off the ground, weeping to see himself in such danger as man lives in. And when there came many people to see him in his cell out of curiosity for the great change that had come over him, and asked the reason of this novelty and of the extreme course he had so suddenly taken, he never answered anything else but: 'Let me alone, because I am a man.' Another saint used to say: 'Woe is me, because I am still capable of offending God mortally.' " Cf. authorized American edition, translated by Joseph Rickaby (Chicago:

pessimistic view of human nature, only intensified the situation.[1] Though St. Vincent reacted against the Jansenists and became their staunch opponent, particularly after the death of his friend, the Abbé de Saint-Cyran,[2] he too breathed the air that they did. Much of what he says to the missionaries about chastity has a negative tone, even when he is attempting to lay out positive motivation for living it.[3]

To encourage the confreres, Vincent notes that Jesus loved chastity deeply and desired that the hearts of his followers be filled with it. He willed to be born of a virgin through the power of the Holy Spirit, contrary to the laws of nature, in order to show his great esteem for chastity. He so appreciated this virtue that, though he allowed himself to be accused falsely of many things, he never let his chastity be questioned.[4]

Vincent often urges on the confreres the importance of growing in chastity and of using prudent precautions, because their work on the missions obliges them to continual contact with lay people of both sexes.[5] In his letters he treats a number of practical cases that came up pastorally. He tells the confreres: to be very slow to ask questions about sexual matters in confession;[6] not to touch women under any pretext whatsoever, not even to touch the pulse of a sick woman to see if it is time to give the last sacraments;[7] to be particularly careful in mission lands because of the different sexual mores of the people there;[8] and not to have women as workers in our houses.[9]

In the Rules and in his conferences, he adds a number of practical directives:

Loyola University, 1929) III, 272. This enormously popular book, published originally at Seville in 1609 and read in many Vincentian novitiates over more than three centuries, is actually less negative than some other writings from the period. Interestingly, St. Vincent (cf. CR IV, 1) uses the same motive expressed by Rodriguez at the beginning of the latter's treatment of chastity: "So pleasing to God is this virtue that, when the Son of God became man and had to be born of a woman, he chose to be born of a virgin mother, and one consecrated by a vow of chastity, as the saints observe." Cf. III, 227.

1. Cf. Román, 602-604. Román notes the contrast between Jansenism's pessimism in regard to human nature and St. Vincent's vision of the poor person as the image of Christ.
2. Cf. the very interesting account of Vincent's change in attitude after 1643, in A. Dodin, La Légende et L'Histoire de Monsieur Depaul à saint Vincent de Paul (Paris, 1985) 168.
3. On the other hand, at times St. Vincent speaks quite positively about the spousal relationship between Christ and the Daughter of Charity who pronounces vows. Cf. SV X, 169-70; also X, 618-20.
4. CR IV, 1. St. Vincent comments on this paragraph of the rule in his conference of December 12, 1659; cf. SV XII, 412-24.
5. SV XI, 166. Cf. also SV XI, 209; XII, 416-17.
6. SV I, 547.
7. SV II, 523: "You must be on your guard against using this practice, which the evil spirit can employ to tempt the living as well as the dying. . . ."
8. SV III, 282: "I know how much your heart loves purity," he writes to Charles Nacquart. "You will have to work hard at it there . . . ."
9. SV IV, 313.

- they should keep careful control of their exterior senses (sight, smell, taste, touch, hearing), as well as their interior senses (understanding, memory, will);[1]
- they should never be alone with a woman at an inappropriate time or place;[2]
- in talking with or writing to women, they should completely avoid language that is too tender and affectionate; and in speaking with women within or outside confession, they should not get too close;[3]
- they should drink very little wine and have it well watered;[4]
- they should not direct women religious,[5] nor be in the frequent company of the Daughters of Charity, nor enter their rooms;[6]
- they should not give Missions to nuns, nor receive letters from them under the pretext of giving needed advice.[7]
- they should never presume on their chastity.[8]

St. Vincent warns about two vices which are enemies of chastity: intemperance and idleness. He calls intemperance "the nursing mother of unchastity"[9] and urges the members of the Company to be moderate in what they eat and drink and to use plain foods. He describes idleness as "the enemy of virtue, especially of chastity"[10] and recommends that they always be usefully occupied.[11]

On the positive side, humility is an excellent means for acquiring and maintaining chastity.[12] So also is frequent prayer to Our Lord, the Blessed Virgin,[13] and the saints.[14]

Missionaries should live this virtue to such a degree that people will not

---

1. Cf. SV IX, 23; X, 59; X, 246; X, 280; X, 399; XII, 215, on the exterior senses, and X, 151; X, 246; X, 280, on the interior senses. Cf. also SV XI, 209; XII, 418f.
2. Cf. SV XII, 419.
3. SV XII, 421.
4. SV XI, 167
5. *Ibid.* After giving this directive, St. Vincent holds a wonderful dialogue with himself. " 'Yes, Sir,' someone may say to me, 'But you certainly do so yourself.' I reply that the Blessed Francis de Sales charged me with the direction of the convent of the Visitation in this city. . . ." He then describes all his efforts (unsuccessful ones!) to get out of this job.
6. SV XI, 168.
7. *Ibid.*
8. CR IV, 2.
9. CR IV, 3.
10. CR IV, 5.
11. Cf. SV XII, 420.
12. SV XI, 168.
13. Cf. SV XI, 220-21, where St. Vincent is speaking to the Daughters: "Saying the rosary is a very beautiful devotion, especially for the Daughters of Charity, who have such a great need for God's help in order to have the kind of purity that is so necessary for them."
14. SV XI, 209: "Let us ask him for this grace. My heart tells me that if we ask him for it earnestly he will have mercy on us."

have even the slightest suspicion about their chastity. Even an unjust suspicion will cause grave harm to the work of the mission, so missionaries should take not just ordinary, but even extraordinary, means to prevent such damage. Consequently, it might be necessary for them to abstain even from some good work if, in the judgment of the superior, it will give rise to suspicions of this sort.[1]

Practice modifying theory

But if the Rules and conferences have a rather negative ring, Vincent manifests little of this negativity in his own relationship with women. He interpreted the Rules *modo humano*.

He speaks with great tenderness about many of the women whom he knew and worked closely with, especially Madame de Gondi,[2] Marguerite Naseau,[3] Jane de Chantal,[4] and Louise de Marillac.[5] He was the personal friend of the Queen of France (Ann of Austria) and the Queen of Poland (Marie de Gonzague) and a close collaborator with a very large number of Ladies of Charity. His correspondence with St. Louise is strikingly warm. He writes to her in October 1627: "I am writing to you at about midnight and am a little tired. Forgive my heart if it is not a little more expansive in this letter. Be faithful to your faithful lover who is Our Lord. Also be very simple and humble. And I shall be, in the love of Our Lord and his holy mother . . . ."[6] Again, on New Year's Day, 1638, he writes:

I wish you a young heart and a love in its first bloom for him Who loves us unceasingly and as tenderly as if he were just beginning to love us. For all God's pleasures are ever new and full of variety, although he never changes. I am, in his love, with an affection such as his Goodness desires and which I owe him out of love for him, Mademoiselle, your most humble servant . . .[7]

His letters also contain much concrete, direct advice to those who are troubled. To a brother who wanted to become a Carthusian in order to escape temptations against chastity, he writes: "Of this I assure you: if you are not continent in the Mission, you will not be so anywhere in the world."[8] He also

---

1. CR IV, 4.
2. Cf., especially, SV III, 97.
3. Cf., especially, SV IX, 77.
4. Cf., especially, SV XIII, 125.
5. Cf., especially, SV X, 709; XIII, 695; cf. also A. Dodin, "San Vicente y la mujer en la vida de la iglesia," in *Lecciones sobre Vicencianismo* (CEME, 1977) 173-176.
6. SV I, 30.
7. SV I, 417-18.
8. SV IV, 592-93; cf. also III, 348.

recommends that the brother avoid contact with the person who gave rise to the temptation and that he speak about the problem in spiritual direction. To a priest at Saint-Meen, who was depressed because of troublesome thoughts, he writes: "Your depression will not last. It is like a thick cloud that passes. Man is like the weather, which never stays the same . . . ." He urges this priest to speak openly with his superior, who "is a good missionary, wise and virtuous."[1] He encourages another priest who is plagued with temptations: "You should not be surprised that you suffer temptations. It is a trial that God sends you to humble you and arouse fear in you. But have confidence in him. His grace will be sufficient, provided that you avoid the occasions. . . . Develop the habit of letting your heart rest in the sacred wounds of Christ. That is a refuge that is inaccessible to the enemy."[2]

Perhaps most striking of all, and filled with common sense, is the wonderfully warm letter St. Vincent wrote to Jacques Tholard on February 1, 1640. It is a masterpiece of practical moral reasoning combined with compassionate pastoral judgment. Tholard, who was later Visitor of the Province of France and that of Lyons, found himself plagued with temptations while hearing confessions. St. Vincent writes to him:

> That is why the masters of the spiritual life think that these happenings which occur in confession are not sins at all, and do not require in our day that they be confessed. . . . It would be well for you to pass over these matters as lightly as you can. That is the first piece of advice that is usually given, and that one be not troubled when one feels too much pleasure. The second is to try to turn your eyes away from the faces and the other parts of the body of the female sex that cause the temptation. And when the opposite happens, be assured, Monsieur, that it will be when you are not free and your will is weakened by the strength of the temptation. And do not be troubled when you think that is not so.[3]

---

1. SV V, 614.
2. SV VIII, 429.
3. SV II, 15-17. But this letter should be read in the English language version; cf. *Vincent de Paul. Correspondence, Conferences, Documents*, Vol. II (New York: New City Press, 1990) 19-23. Unfortunately, Coste omits, as does the translation contained in the Spanish edition, many portions of this letter which make very explicit reference to sexual matters.

3. Obedience

His teaching

As he did consistently, St. Vincent uses the example of Our Lord as a primary motive when he addresses the priests and brothers about obedience. Jesus, he tells them, obeyed not only Mary and Joseph, but others in positions of authority, both the good and the bad. He constantly submitted himself to his Father's will, even to death. In fact, his whole life was "nothing but a web of obedience."[1]

In the Rules, Vincent tells the members of the Congregation that they must obey the pope and the bishops of the dioceses in which they work;[2] nor should they do anything in parish churches without the consent of the pastor.[3] They should likewise obey the Superior General "promptly, joyfully, and perseveringly"[4] in all matters that are not clearly sinful.[5] With a certain blind obedience, they should submit their judgment[6] and their will not only to his judgment, but even to his intention. They should always think that what he commands is better and should place themselves at his disposal like a file in the hands of a carpenter.

They owe this same kind of obedience to Visitors, local superiors and other subordinate officials.[7]

They shall also strive to obey the bell as the voice of Christ and respond as soon as they hear it, leaving even a letter of the alphabet unfinished if they are writing.[8]

His letters and conferences make it evident that Vincent attaches great importance to obedience.[9] He tells Lambert aux Couteaux: "I am a child of obedience. It seems to me that, if he (the bishop) should tell me to go to the far end of his diocese and stay there for the rest of my life, I would do it as

---

1. SV XII, 426. St. Vincent comments on the paragraphs in the Common Rules concerning obedience in his conference of December 19, 1659 (SV XII, 424-33).
2. Cf. also SV III, 38-39: "How can you know the will of God in temporal matters better than by the will of the princes, and in spiritual matters than by that of our lords, the bishops, each in his own diocese."
3. CR V, 1.
4. CR V, 2.
5. SV XII, 429.
6. In a conference to the Daughters, St. Vincent speaks very forcefully about submitting their judgment; cf. SV X, 390.
7. CR V, 3.
8. *Ibid.*
9. One could give a large number of examples. Cf. SV III, 301, on obedience to the doctor; III, 343, on obedience to the queen. For the Daughter of Charity, obedience is her cloister (IX, 513-14). It enables her to go anywhere in the service of the poor (X, 128).

if Our Lord had commanded me, and whatever solitude or job he would give me there would be a foretaste of paradise, since I would be doing the good pleasure of God."[1]

For Vincent, obedience involves profound renunciation of judgment and will, and is part of the overall gospel call to self-denial in the following of Christ.[2]

In order to grow in obedience, missionaries shall develop the habit of "indifference,"[3] by observing the Congregation's long-standing custom of "asking for nothing and refusing nothing."[4] But if, before God, they really think that something is necessary or, conversely, is doing some harm, they shall lay the matter before the superior. When this has been done, they shall regard the superior's decision as a certain sign of God's will and shall acquiesce immediately.

To concretize the practice of obedience, St. Vincent lays down a number of rather detailed norms in the Common Rule:

- everyone shall gather at the designated time and place to hear what the superior has to say about house matters; if they have anything to propose, it should be said then;[5]
- no one shall give commands to others nor correct them, unless delegated by the superior or bound to do it by office;[6]
- no one, after being refused something by one superior, shall go to another about the same matter without telling him about the refusal and the reasons for it;[7]
- even if some legitimate business should arise, no one should abandon some task that has been committed to him, without first telling the superior, so that, if necessary, a substitute can be found;[8]
- no one shall intrude into the duties or ministries of others; but if asked, he shall help out willingly; if, however, this help will occupy much of his time, he shall first seek the permission of the superior;[9]

---

1. SV I, 511. Cf. also his strong words to Robert de Sergis (I, 554) and Jean Dehorgny (II, 567). The value St. Vincent sees in obedience comes across quite strikingly in his comments to St. Louise. He writes to her: "Just as a beautiful diamond is worth more than a mountain of stones, so also, an act of compliance and submission is worth more than a number of good works done for others" (SV I, 482). Later, seeing the bad state of her health, he tells her to stay at home, adding that her obedience will be worth more before God than the Mass she wants to attend (SV IV, 182).
2. SV XII, 427f.
3. Cf. CR II, 3.
4. CR V, 4.
5. CR V, 5.
6. CR V, 6.
7. CR V, 7.
8. CR V, 8.
9. CR V, 9.

- no one shall write or send letters, or open letters he has received, without the permission of the superior; when a confrere writes a letter, he shall give it to the superior, who will, as he sees fit, either send it or not;[1]
- without general or special permission, no one shall enter another's room nor even open it unless the other invites him to come in; they will leave the door open while together;[2]
- no one will let others, especially outsiders, into his room without the permission of the superior;[3]
- no one shall enter the place set aside for another's ministry (his office, for example) without the permission of the superior or the one in charge of the place;[4]
- no one shall write a book or translate and publish one, without the expressed permission of the Superior General;[5]
- brothers[6] shall not aspire to study Latin nor to become clerics; they shall not learn to read or write without the expressed permission of the Superior General;[7]
- as a means toward better health, no one shall eat or drink, outside the usual times, without the permission of the superior;[8]
- the sick should obey their doctors and those taking care of them.[9]

Practice modifying theory

While St. Vincent firmly recommended obedience to all superiors, especially to the pope, he was sometimes dogged in trying to get what he wanted, particularly if he thought it vital to the future of his Company. He held steadfast to the interests of the Congregation in the face of resistance on the part of authorities, curial politics, or bureaucratic inertia.

---

1. CR V, 11.
2. CR V, 13.
3. CR V, 14.
4. CR V, 10.
5. CR V, 15; cf. also his letter to François du Coudray, who was seeking permission to remain in Rome to translate the Syriac Bible into Latin: "Picture to yourself then, sir, that there are millions of souls with outstretched hands calling you . . . !" (SV I, 252).
6. As the recent draft-document entitled "Brothers of the Mission" (sent to the Visitors on April 15, 1989) points out, St. Vincent, "influenced at times by the attitudes of his era about brothers in religious and apostolic communities but guided at other times by his own instincts about the need to respect persons and evaluate them as they really are, frequently comes across admirably to us, but sometimes is also disconcerting."
7. CR V, 16.
8. CR V, 12.
9. CR VI, 3.

This is quite evident in his efforts to obtain approval for the vows to be pronounced in the Congregation. And in fact, he was successful in getting his way! "In Rome," he states, quoting Commander de Sillery, "everything can be achieved with time and patience."[1] He encourages René Alméras, his negotiator in Rome:[2] "This is a cloud that will pass. The day will come when the Company will be more acceptable and when those who can do good for it will have more charity toward it than they now have."

He even forwarded to Alméras Cardinal Grimaldi's suggestion to use a little money to facilitate negotiations! But he regretted having done this. He thanks Alméras for having opposed him on the matter and adds, "I wrote that crooked proposition to you only because it was suggested to me by Cardinal Grimaldi, and once more I assure you that I am very edified that you refused it."[3]

"Get the bulls at any price and in the best possible form," he tells Edme Jolly in 1658.[4]

In fact, he came to regard careful negotiations with authorities as one of the ways of honoring providence. He writes to Edme Jolly in Rome in 1658:[5] "You are one of the few men who honor the providence of God more by the preparation of remedies against foreseen evils. I thank you very humbly for this and pray that Our Lord will continue to enlighten you more and more so that such enlightenment may spread through the Company." It is also evident from his correspondence with Jolly that he wanted him to be firm in pressing his points with the Sacred Congregation of Propaganda Fide.[6]

He could also be quite firm with bishops who made demands that were contrary to the practice of the Congregation (e.g., that missionaries submit an account of their financial affairs to the local ordinary). Only ten days before his death, he writes to the Archbishop of Narbonne, who was seeking both the right to look at the accounts and to dismiss members of the Congregation from the seminary staff: "Your Excellency would greatly oblige us if you drew up the deed of agreement in the same way as the other French and Italian bishops have done."[7]

---

1. SV XIII, 336.
2. SV III, 453.
3. SV III, 486.
4. SV III, 247.
5. SV VII, 310.
6. SV VII, 331.
7. SV VIII, 451.

4. Stability

His teaching

The reader will look in vain for an extended treatment of stability in the Common Rules or in the extant conferences of St. Vincent, though he does often speak of Christ's using the "weapons" of poverty, chastity, and obedience "even to death" and of the need for the missionary to persevere "even to death."[1]

Yet stability is at the root of much of what St. Vincent thought, said and wrote about the vows. It pains him deeply that some of the best missionaries leave.[2] Perseverance, he tells Fr. Alméras, is one of the principal motives for his seeking to have the members of the Company pronounce vows.[3] He felt very strongly about the matter. "There is no better way to assure our eternal happiness than to live and die in the service of the poor within the arms of providence and in a real renunciation of ourselves by following Jesus Christ," he writes to Jean Barreau on December 4, 1648.[4]

On October 16, 1658, he wrote to two confreres, both in the house at Troyes, who were experiencing vocational struggles. He tells Jacques de la Fosse: "When we think about another state of life, we picture for ourselves only what is pleasant in it, but when we are actually there, we experience only what is troublesome in it and what runs contrary to nature. Remain in peace, Father, and continue your voyage to heaven in the boat in which God has placed you. That is what I hope from his goodness and from the desire which you have to do his Will."[5] To Jacques Tholard, he further states: "If you have succeeded in remaining for twenty years in the Company, you will remain yet another twenty or thirty years in it, since things will not be more difficult in the future than they were in the past. In binding yourself to God exactly as the others do, not only will you edify them, but Our Lord will bind himself more closely than ever to you, and he will be your strength in your weakness; he will be your joy in your sorrow; and he will be your stability in your wavering."[6]

It is evident that, even in St. Vincent's lifetime, missionaries who did not

---

1. Cf. CR II, 18.
2. SV I, 551: "I have just now seen a member of the Company, one of the very best among us . . . who is determined to leave . . . without giving me any particular reason."
3. SV III, 379-80.
4. SV III, 392. St. Vincent speaks equally strongly with the Daughters of Charity (SV IX, 625-26): "Without perseverance, everything is lost. . . ." Cf. also IX, 637: "The one who does not persevere to the end does not receive a reward."
5. SV VII, 292-92.
6. SV VII, 294.

work directly with the poor, but rather in seminaries, felt some tension in regard to this vow, since it was formulated in terms of dedicating oneself, for the whole time of one's life, to the salvation of the poor country people. In 1654 Vincent responds to a question posed by François Fournier, saying that such confreres fulfill their vow, first of all, by holding themselves ready to go to the poor at the slightest indication and, secondly, by working for the poor indirectly since they are forming good priests who will themselves then go to the poor.[1]

In various contexts, St. Vincent speaks of diverse "enemies" of perseverance in the Company, especially the failure to rise early,[2] lack of prayer,[3] and neglect of the practice of poverty.[4]

Practice modifying theory

St. Vincent was very eager that good confreres keep their commitments. He sometimes pleaded with them to stay or to return. In 1646, in a remarkable letter to Thomas Berthe, he makes an eloquent appeal:[5] "Come back, Father. I conjure you by the promise you made to God to live and die in the Company. . . ." The following month he makes a further plea: "I will have more confidence in you than ever (if you come back), because I will no longer be afraid of losing you, having seen you saved from such a dangerous reef. Choose any house you please. You will be received everywhere with open arms. . . ."[6]

But in fact, he was sometimes happy when other confreres left. He tells René Alméras that we should regard the departure of some persons as something good for the Congregation.[7] In his diary, Jean Gicquel describes St. Vincent's reaction (just eight days before his death) when Achille LeVazeux departed: " 'O my Savior, what a grace you have given us in unloading someone like him, brilliant to the point of pride and haughtiness!' . . . Fr. Vincent for the next four or five days repeated several times at each meeting: 'What a reason for thanking God for having delivered us. . . !' "[8]

Similarly, it is evident that he was glad to let Chrétien Daisne leave[9] and was more than eager to get rid of Brother Doutrelet, whose departure, he

---

1. SV V, 81.
2. SV III, 538; IX, 29; X, 566.
3. SV III, 539; IX, 416; X, 583; XI, 83.
4. SV XI, 79, 223.
5. SV III, 88.
6. SV III, 118.
7. SV III, 379.
8. SV XIII, 186-87.
9. SV VII, 354.

states, God will use "to make the Congregation survive."[1] When five con-freres left in 1642 and two were expelled, he reflects on the event in a letter to François Dufestel,[2] saying, "this kind would hurt us more in the battle than they would help."

Nor, failing to find sufficient reason to dispense a troublesome student confrere from his vows, was he loath to suggest putting pressure on him, hoping that he might change his ways, but foreseeing that he might leave.[3] He suggests depriving him of wine at table or even locking him in a room!

As one might expect, he was even more decisive in dismissing those not yet in vows. "We have purged and re-purged the seminary," he tells Jean Dehorgny while informing him that thirty remained in the internal seminary.[4] But later, in 1657, he admonishes the director of the seminary for being too harsh.[5] He seems quite concerned that directors be realistic in their expectations and that they lead the seminarists step by step.[6]

---

1. SV III, 379.
2. SV II, 287.
3. SV VII, 210: ". . . it will be a relief for it (the Congregation) to be rid of someone incorrigible."
4. SV II, 489. The number of seminarists was rather large at that time. Two years earlier St. Vincent mentioned that there were 36 or 38, adding (II, 323): "I think that Our Lord grants this because he sees in the Congregation some determination in purging the incorrigible."
5. SV VI, 385-88.
6. SV V 436-37.

PART II - HORIZON-SHIFTS BETWEEN
THE SEVENTEENTH AND TWENTIETH CENTURIES

In the last chapter, when discussing the five characteristic virtues, I briefly described six horizon-shifts that have taken place between the seventeenth and twentieth centuries, which inevitably influence the way we look at St. Vincent's teaching today: 1) a change in philosophical and theological methodology; 2) increasing consciousness of interdependence; 3) a changed paradigm for the exercise of authority; 4) emphasis on a Christology and an ecclesiology "from below"; 5) a shift toward a more positive attitude in regard to creation and toward less emphasis on sin; 6) a transition from the "era of Christendom" to the "era of the secular." Here, I will further develop the notion of "horizon-shifts" and will describe briefly some additional ways in which modern thought-processes have changed since the time of St. Vincent.

Horizon-shifts, whether we react to them favorably or unfavorably, necessarily have an impact on the way we interpret reality. If we look out on a broad plain from a vantage-point half-way up a mountain, we see more of it than we did while on the ground, though we may see it in less detail. If we climb to the top of the mountain, the vista may broaden further: we might view the entire plain or we might even be able to see over the top of the next mountain; still, we may also no longer be able to distinguish some of the people below, or the buildings, or the trees nearly so clearly as we did when we were lower on the mountain. But if we descend to the foot of the mountain again, we can see nothing of what lies beyond the next series of mountains nor can we see much of the plain; yet we do see the nearby people, buildings and trees quite clearly. And from down below, we might even have a better view of the mountainside than when we were actually on it.

As is obvious from the metaphor, horizon-shifts bear with them losses and gains. Sometimes the gains vastly outweigh the losses; sometimes, vice-versa. But inevitably they affect our way of interpreting reality.

As we attempt to interpret the meaning of St. Vincent's teaching on the vows and seek to reinterpret it today, it is imperative that we be aware of the horizon-shifts that have taken place since the seventeenth century. Otherwise, the Vincent de Paul that we offer to others will be merely a still photo from the past, rather than a living, relevant teacher; or, a corpse rather than vibrant saint.

At the heart of interpretation is meaning. We must attempt to find the meaning of St. Vincent's teaching as he presented it in a seventeenth-century form and express it in twentieth-century forms which will be capable of mediating it to our contemporaries (but, first of all, to ourselves). Of course, not all seventeenth-century forms are irrelevant today; many practices which St. Vincent suggested are still apt means for expressing the values he sought. Yet, just as many languages cease to exist as a living word capable of communicating meaning, so also some of the practices that were once suitable vehicles for expressing values in St. Vincent's time are no longer capable of doing so now. In those cases, the challenge is to find or create new forms that will do the job.[1]

A preparatory document,[2] meant to stimulate discussion for the 1990 Synod, mentioned a number of significant changes in mentality that inevitably affect us today, both for good and for bad. In a similar vein, I will here briefly touch on several horizon-shifts,[3] in addition to those described in the last chapter, which have an impact on the way we view the vows.

As I write about horizon-shifts, I am conscious of an enormous limitation. Not everyone living at the same historical moment lives in the same "world."[4] Horizons vary greatly from east to west and from north to south. The cultural, philosophical, and theological backgrounds of people living in India, for example, are significantly different from those living in Europe or North America.[5] Nonetheless, recognizing this limitation, I offer these thoughts,

---

1. Putting all this in traditional language, one might say that the challenge is to find the substance of the four vows, to put aside those concrete ("accidental") forms that are no longer appropriate for mediating that substance in the modern world, and to find contemporary forms which will embody it more readily. In his essays on spirituality, Karl Rahner suggests the distinction between "material" and "formal" imitation of Christ. In the former, one focuses on the concrete things that Jesus did and tries to do them, without realizing the extent to which everything he did was conditioned by his historical context. In "formal" imitation, one seeks to find the core or meaning of what Jesus said or did and then seeks to apply that in the contemporary context. Other writers distinguish between "imitation of Christ" (which tends to emphasize "material" imitation) and the "following of Christ" (which tends to emphasize "formal" imitation).

2. *Lineamenta*, "The Formation of Priests in Circumstances of the Present Day," for the use of Episcopal Conferences, in preparation for the Synod of 1990 (Vatican City, 1989) 10-11. Among the changes which it describes is the "modern character" of western culture, with its rejection of absolute norms, a tendency to reduce all things to technology, and widespread secularization.

3. For an interesting account of major shifts in contemporary society, cf. Joseph J. Hayden, "Megatrends of Human Development," *Human Development* 5 (1984) 11-14; also J. Naisbitt, *Megatrends: Ten New Directions Transforming Our Lives* (New York: Warner Books, 1982).

4. Cf. *Lineamenta* #5: "The unique aspects of the socio-cultural environment in relation to the different 'worlds' must be considered as well as their impact on formation and on the exercise of mission. Even if the changes of the western world affect other parts of the world through the influence of the mass-media and the migration of peoples, these 'worlds' nevertheless still retain some of their own qualities." Cf. also #29.

5. The problem is actually more complex because, as Karl Rahner points out, not even all those living in the same place at the same time are really "contemporaries."

writing from my own time and place in history, attempting to make adjustments based on my limited knowledge of other cultures, and trusting that others will complete the task for their own cultures.

It is also important to point out that horizon-shifts, especially of the sweeping Copernican type, only slowly take root within the minds of those living at a given point in history. Old paradigms die slowly. To the end of their lives, some persons will continue to act and react as if no change at all has taken place.[1]

Let me describe briefly here a few additional horizon-shifts that are relevant for our study of the vows.

1. The transition from an industrial society to an information society

Since the time of St. Vincent, the western world has witnessed the transition from an agrarian to an industrial to an information society. The last-mentioned change, toward a society based largely on the creation and distribution of information, is still very much in process today. It brings with it lights and shadows, gifts and burdens.

On the one hand, advances in communication provide the opportunity for the rapid dissemination of information. Computers enable us to solve in seconds problems that formerly cost us months of work or were even insoluble. Television instantaneously brings events and entertainment right into the living-room.

But the blessing has sometimes been a very mixed one. The same information that enables society to save lives also enables it to destroy them. Nor does every form of entertainment beamed into the community recreation room or the local theater really "build up the Body of Christ." Much discernment is needed. The information explosion challenges society as a whole, and religious communities in particular, to reflective, responsible, critical moral thinking. Not everything that can be done *should* be done; not everything that can be produced *should* be produced.

In an information society, moreover, the demands on those in authority are great. People want to know what is happening. They want to have their say in it. And they know that the means for both are available.

But while "high technology" (especially through computerization) makes more and more advances, "high touch" in governance and relationships is

---

1. Cf. Thomas Kuhn, The *Structure of Scientific Revolutions* (Chicago: University of Chicago Press, 1962).

also more and more in demand. Perhaps even *because* so much of life and work has become impersonalized, people seek deeper human relationships. They want to see and talk with their superiors face to face.[1] They call for a community life that is not merely functional, but personal.

All this presents enormous challenges for those living community life, especially for those in authority.

2. The movement from national economies toward a world economy

The writings of John XXIII, Paul VI, and John Paul II have been marked by a strong emphasis on the need for a global world-view. Social encyclicals and the writings of many bishops criticize the ever-widening gap between the rich nations and the poor nations. Economic policy based predominantly on nationalism[2] is viewed as an enemy of the global community.

This changing perspective creates extremely complex challenges for society. On the international level, the need for a more just "international economic order" is often spoken of. An individual nation cannot just consider its own economic goals in isolation from the community of nations. People are, moreover, increasingly conscious that short-range planning must give way to longer-range views and that the short-sighted resolution of one problem (e.g., the need for energy) sometimes produces even greater ones (e.g., the pollution of the air, the rivers, the sea).

In the politico-economic order, the need to enter the world economy has clearly been one of the principal factors in the recent literal breakdown of the wall dividing East and West. The nations of Eastern Europe are struggling to integrate themselves into and share in a world economy.

Naturally, this movement creates challenges for religious communities too. Those dedicated to the poor recognize that short-term assistance to a poor person, while necessary, does not really get to the heart of the matter. There are unjust social structures that keep poor people poor. Consequently, there is a demand for social analysis. It is in this light that John Paul II called the members of the Congregation of the Mission, during the General Assembly of 1986, to "search out more than ever, with boldness, humility and skill, the causes of poverty and encourage long and short term solutions, which are concrete, flexible and efficacious."[3]

Congregations are also conscious that the investment of their funds not

---

1. Cf. G. Arbuckle, *Out of Chaos* (New York: Paulist, 1988) 41.
2. I distinguish here between nationalism and a healthy patriotism.
3. Cf. Lines of Action #8.

only has implications for the community's future, but also has a moral, and sometimes economic, impact on society as a whole. As a result, numerous religious communities have established advisory boards which review their investments and make recommendations on how to exercise their voting power as stock holders, or subscribe to international or regional services which do this.

Many congregations too are increasingly conscious of their international character, with the varied cultures, languages, religious backgrounds, economic and political systems of their members. Dialogue and decision-making in such a context are experienced as highly delicate processes. The problem becomes all the more complicated when some provinces are perceived as "rich" and others as "poor."

3. The shift from North to South

During the fifteen-year pontificate of Paul VI, a striking shift took place in the Church's statistical center of gravity. The turning point arrived in 1970: fifty-one percent of the Catholic population was living in the southern continents. By the year 2,000, seventy percent of all Catholics will be in the southern hemisphere.[1] Walbert Bühlmann calls this the "coming of the third Church."[2]

In an existential sense, Catholicism is becoming truly a "world-church," as Karl Rahner pointed out on many occasions.[3]

Many religious communities are experiencing this dramatically. In our own Congregation, for example, while there are fewer vocations in western Europe and North America, where formerly they flourished, the Company is growing not only in Poland, but also in the Philippines, India, Indonesia, Colombia, Mexico, Central America, Ethiopia, Nigeria, Zaire, Mozambique and Madagascar.

For the Congregation, the opportunities and the challenges are enormous. The confreres from these countries enrich the Congregation with their own cultures and religious traditions. They often, for example, bring us an experience of life lived out continually in intimate contact with the poor. Such provinces frequently have active, even thriving, programs for mini-

---

1. W. Bühlmann, *The Church of the Future* (Maryknoll, New York: Orbis, 1986) 4-5.
2. Cf. W. Bühlmann, *The Coming of the Third Church* (Slough, England: St. Paul Publications, 1976).
3. K. Rahner, "The Abiding Significance of the Second Vatican Council," in *Theological Investigations* XX, 90-102; cf. also "The Future of the Church and the Church of the Future," in *Theological Investigations* XX, 103-14.

sterial formation among both the clergy and the laity. But they also express two striking needs: 1) the need for trained personnel to carry on the work of our own formation; 2) the need for further inculturation, so that the Christianity and culture might interact with one another at a deeper level, both enriching and purifying each other. Rahner points out that the *globalization* of theology is one of the greatest needs of the Church in the years ahead. He notes that up to the present there has been an unfortunate tendency to "canonize" what was really only a manifestation of the thought patterns of western culture.[1]

Right now, many growing, younger provinces, and particularly those responsible for formation within them, face the difficult challenge of teaching philosophy and theology (so often formulated in a European or North American context) in an African or Asian or South American or Pacific Island setting. Similarly, they search for the appropriate forms for expressing poverty, chastity, obedience, and life-long commitment to the poor within cultures very different not only from St. Vincent's, but also from those of the writers of most of the philosophy, theology, and spiritual reading books written up until recent times.

Along these same lines, the place of women in society and the social mores in relating to them vary greatly from north to south and, in both hemispheres, from continent to continent. To talk with a woman on the street may be as "natural" in Los Angeles as it is "scandalous" in Mecca.

4. Further changes in the paradigms for exercising authority

The discontent that until recently pulsated mostly beneath the surface in China, Russia, Poland, and most of Eastern Europe has now exploded dramatically. Through both peaceful and violent means, people are seeking, and obtaining, greater voice in their own governments.

In a more orderly way (though the experience was sometimes also quite dramatic), the Church has been experiencing a similar phenomenon over the past three decades. In the last chapter, I briefly described the shift from a monarchical to a collegial model of authority in the Church. This paradigm-shift is still very much in process. In community life, it is taking a number of concrete shapes.

One can note, first, a movement from the desire for representation to the desire for participation. With the possibility of rapid communication, people are often not satisfied with decision-making processes that involve just the

---

1. Cf. citation in Bühlmann, *The Church of the Future* 193.

provincial and his council or even an elected provincial assembly, especially if the decisions to be made affect the lives of all members of a province intimately. They expect to be consulted personally on all important matters concerning their future. At times too, in matters of major importance, they expect all the members of the province to be consulted. Along these lines, we witness today the development of some rather sophisticated, detailed consultation processes. We also witness the advent of general meetings of the whole province, either alongside or occasionally in place of elected provincial assemblies.

Secondly, alongside hierarchical structures, there is a tendency toward much greater "networking," sometimes at the initiative of the hierarchy itself and sometimes as a result of a call "from below." Much of the networking has already been institutionalized in the Code of Canon Law (diocesan synods, presbyteral councils, pastoral councils, etc.) and in the Constitutions, Statutes, and Provincial Norms of various communities (assemblies, house meetings, local community plans, provincial plans, etc.).

Thirdly, contemporary society offers fewer either/or choices but, rather, proposes multiple options. Such options are often a product of the information society and of advanced technology, which has the capacity to propose and explore different possibilities. Groups, as they begin long-range planning, often speak today of various "scenarios," based on different hypotheses. In religious communities too, the exploration of multiple options is now a frequent part of life, especially in consultation concerning future assignments. Moreover, interest surveys of all the confreres of a province are often used as a tool in planning for the future.

Lest the reader be overwhelmed by the magnitude of the changes described above, it may be helpful to note the comment of a contemporary writer:

> *In some ways, persons directly serving the Church are better prepared for the megatrends than the average person, because they have not been employed by industry but rather have been working in service-related occupations that can be more easily integrated into an information society. Furthermore, if they have been active in the Roman Catholic Church during the past twenty years, they already have experienced major changes.*[1]

---

1. Hayden, 14.

PART III - THE FOUR VINCENTIAN VOWS RETRIEVED

In this section I will follow the order used in article 28 of the Constitutions and in the Program for Vincentian Formation in the Major Seminary;[1] the sequence employed in these more recent documents is different from that of the Common Rules and reflects, at least to some extent, a different perspective on the vows.[2]

In reflecting on each vow, I will offer considerations "toward a contemporary understanding" and "toward a contemporary practice." I am eager to stimulate further dialogue and writing "toward" such an understanding and practice. But in doing so, I am aware, as many recent documents point out, that such theoretical considerations will have a genuine life-giving influence on others, especially on those in formation, only if they are accompanied by the witness of wise, healthy role-models, whose lives speak more forcefully than their teaching.[3]

As a final preliminary remark, let me note here (so as not to repeat it again and again) the importance of two factors in re-interpreting the vows today. Both are strongly emphasized in contemporary Church documents and both were of enormous importance to St. Vincent: 1) the missionary dimension of the vows, which has received much attention since *Evangelii Nuntiandi*; and, 2) the Church's preferential option for the poor and her prophetic call to justice in solidarity with them. A contemporary writer expresses the latter point in this way:

So crucial is this issue of justice for the poor that the revitalization of religious life cannot be considered today, if there is no concern for the exploited and the "little people" of this world. Religious are to be more radical Christians, in the sense of struggling to live the life and holiness of the Church in all its radicalness and integrity. There can be no radicalness without concern for the poor.[4]

---

1. The order used in art. 28 of the Constitutions changes in articles 29-39, where stability is placed last.
2. The order for considering the vows, however, is really quite disputable (and of relatively minor importance). Historically, it has been quite varied. Cf. *Lineamenta* #12, for a different order.
3. Cf. Program for Vincentian Formation in the Major Seminary, #53-54. Cf. *Lineamenta* #19.
4. Arbuckle, *Ibid.* 67.

1. Stability

Toward a contemporary understanding[1]

a. In the earliest days of religious life[2] (as well as in the first three years or so of the Congregation[3]), there were no explicit vows.

At the beginning of the history of religious life, a person was incorporated into a community when he made a deliberate decision to enter the particular group, was received (after some probation) by a superior, and was clothed in the religious habit. A simple, stark ceremony that embraced these three elements expressed the person's willingness to renounce everything for the Lord's sake and for the sake of his kingdom. There were no vows, but rather a single, underlying commitment (expressed in the simple ceremony of reception): explicit, total dedication to the Lord and his service, as lived out in the life of the community. Implicitly this involved living a life of chastity, poverty, and obedience.

We might call this primitive, underlying reality, which lies at the heart of religious life, "the one vow" (which later became explicitated into three or four vows). At its core lies: 1) single-minded focus on the Lord; 2) firm commitment to the following of Christ, with its radical demands (the willingness to renounce human ties, worldly goods, one's own preferences, even

---

1. Perhaps the best contemporary study of the history and theology of vows and religious life is by J. Lozano, *Discipleship: Towards an Understanding of Religious Life*, tr. by B. Wilczynski (Chicago/Los Angeles/Manila: Claret Center for Resources in Spirituality, 1980). Cf. also J. Metz, *Followers of Christ: The Religious Life and the Church*, tr. by T. Linton (Ramsey: Paulist, 1978); S. Schneiders, *New Wine-Skins* (New York: Paulist, 1986); L. Boff, *God's Witnesses in the Heart of the World*, tr. by R. Fath (Chicago/Los Angeles/Manila: Claret Center for Resources in Spirituality, 1981); Marcello Azevedo, *Vocation and Mission. The Challenge of Religious Life Today*, translated by J. Diercksmeier (New York: Paulist, 1988). In writing the third part of this chapter I have also profited greatly from the many articles on the vows scattered through K. Rahner's *Theological Investigations* (cf. especially vols. III, VII, VIII, XX).

2. St. Vincent made it quite clear that we are not religious; our secular identity is also most evident in our contemporary documents (cf. C 3 §2). For that reason, I have attempted to avoid using the word "religious" when referring directly to the Congregation. But it is impossible to avoid the word in the broader context of the history of the vows because of their connection with "religious," strictly speaking. Much of the spirit and some of the practices of religious vows apply to us. In this context, it is also important to note what St. Vincent wrote to Jeanne de Chantal in 1639 (I, 562-63): "And because you wish to know what constitutes our humble way of life, I shall tell you then, most worthy Mother . . . that most of us have made the three vows of poverty, chastity and obedience, and a fourth to devote ourselves all our life to the assistance of the poor common people; . . . and that we practice poverty and obedience, and try, by God's mercy, to live in a religious manner, even though we are not religious."

3. Cf. SV V, 458.

one's own life, for the service of the kingdom of God); 3) the primacy of *agape*, a love of friendship and service; 4) faith and hope in the kingdom, with its life that conquers death.

With time, this "one vow," so to speak, came to be concretized in several vows.

This was, on the one hand, a *natural development*. Societies and individuals tend to make more explicit, with the hope of deepening them, commitments that were formerly implicit. So, for example, in some early novitiates, a rule of life was read to the new members and a promise of obedience began to be demanded of them. In the time of Basil we find a public profession of virginity. Later, various triads arise. By the seventh century, in John Climacus, we find mention of professing poverty, chastity and obedience.[1]

But the process was also a *defensive* one, especially in the time of Basil and Benedict. As abuses arose, people were asked to make an explicit profession of what formerly everyone had taken for granted. In that way, no one could say that he did not know what he was getting into!

Seen from this point of view, the three or four vows are really a way of expressing a single underlying reality that is deeper. This helps us understand the role of the vows in the mind of St. Vincent. Basically, he saw them as a way of radicalizing and deepening the missionaries' commitment to follow Christ the Evangelizer of the Poor (the positive function of the vows) and also as a way of stabilizing our commitment to the Company, with its life and its apostolic goals (their defensive function).

b. When examined further, it is evident that the vows also have both an *incarnational* and an *eschatological* thrust.

Looked at from an incarnational perspective, our four vows, as St. Vincent loved to point out, are rooted in the humanity of Christ. By the vow of stability we commit ourselves to follow Christ the Evangelizer of the Poor, as members of the Congregation, for the whole of our lives. The vow of poverty pledges us, with the poor Christ, to share what we have with the poor and to hold all in common with our brothers in community. The celibate life-style provides us the opportunity, as it did Jesus, for greater mobility, time for prayer, and the freedom to serve many brothers and sisters. Obedience in the footsteps of Christ enables us as an apostolic society to seek the will of the Father and to mobilize our forces and concentrate them on our apostolic goals.

Looked at from an eschatological perspective, poverty places us in radical dependence on God, who is the source of all genuine happiness. Celibacy is a sign that we believe in a future that goes beyond family and children.

---

1. Cf. Lozano, 268-70.

Obedience signifies our willingness to be servants of the kingdom. Stability proclaims that there is a meaning to life that goes deeper than the surface, that there is an order of things that reverses the conventional wisdom, that the poor are the rich in the kingdom of God. In this sense, vows often contradict "conventional wisdom." They make us different from the "world," but in doing so they reveal the deepest meaning of the world.

The incarnational and transcendental aspects of the vows cannot be adequately distinguished; consequently, it is a mistake to separate them or, in a spirituality, to neglect the one or the other. Alone, neither fully expresses the meaning of the vows. In fact, the transcendent is expressed only in and through the incarnational, while the incarnational finds its deepest ground and its ultimate goal only in the transcendent.

Because the vows do have a profoundly transcendent dimension, we sometimes describe them as having a sharp "counter-cultural" tendency. This terminology may not be completely accurate, since one of the deepest currents of Catholicism is its continual dialogue and interplay with culture; consequently, in the Catholic tradition the pertinent question regarding a given culture is always: which things are we to honor and cherish, and which are we to counter and deplore?[1] But, apart from the terminology, it is certainly true that those who pronounce vows must squarely face, within the context of their own culture, the renunciation that they involve. In a society where the media frequently promote "instant gratification" in regard to material goods, sexual pleasure, and self-realization, the "delayed gratification" signified by the faithfully-lived vowed life runs very much against the grain, not only of society, but of the individual making the commitment. Vows, therefore, involve an asceticism which we are called to live out in joy as a response to God's gift.

c. Given this background, it is easier to understand why St. Vincent considered stability as so basic.[2] He saw that many generous men came to serve the poor in the Congregation, but he soon experienced that many, faced with difficulties, also left. So for the better part of two decades he labored to introduce a stabilizing element into his confreres' spirituality which would strengthen them in giving not just one or two years to following Christ as the Evangelizer of the Poor, but their whole lives. In that sense, stability was the basic vow for St. Vincent.

d. In describing this commitment, the "Program for Vincentian Formation in the Major Seminary" states that we vow:

---

1. Cf. Margaret O'Brien Steinfels, "The Church and Public Life," *America* 160 (1989), 557-58.
2. For an interesting treatment of this matter, cf. M. Pérez Flores, "El Cuarto Voto de la CM.: La Estabilidad," *Vincentiana* XXVIII (1984) 236-248.

. . . stability, which entails fidelity to God, who call us to commit ourselves to evangelize the poor in the Vincentian community for our whole lives.[1]

Like all vows made in societies within the Church, stability involves fidelity to God, as well as fidelity to a word spoken in the presence of the community. The specific content of this covenanted word is a promise to: 1) evangelize the poor; 2) in the Congregation of the Mission; 3) until death.

Toward a contemporary practice

Today, stability in living out commitments is particularly difficult, not just in religious life but in marriage as well. Many of the societal supports that once reinforced commitments have vanished. Since 1965, large numbers of religious have left their congregations. In recent years this wave of departures has receded somewhat, but a steady, slower stream of withdrawals persists. The reasons why people have left are varied and complex. I must leave it to others to examine them in detail. But apart from the reasons, the fact remains: the challenge of stability is a huge one today.

Later, under celibacy, I will mention six stabilizing factors that are of great help for living out our vowed commitment perseveringly and joyfully. Besides those, let me here mention four other means for growing in stability:

1. Accepting the Lord's love

A number of superiors and those responsible for formation programs today attest that a negative self-image is the root of many of the problems with which members of communities struggle. This being the case, let me suggest that, along with healthy, loving human relationships, acceptance of the Lord's love is a key factor in the self-acceptance that grounds stability. For many, work or achievements or prestigious positions in the community unfortunately play a disproportionate role in their feeling valued personally. But in the long run, genuine self-worth rests on a consciousness of the deep personal love of the Lord as Creator and Redeemer.

Meditation on some striking scriptural texts concerning the Lord's personal love for us is a very helpful means for growing in awareness of that love. In his struggles to be faithful, Moses, pleading for light and strength, heard these words from the Lord (cf. Ex 33:7-17):

This request, too, which you have just made, I will carry out, because you have found favor with me and you are my intimate friend.

---

1. Program #14a; cf. also C 28; 39.

Among many other texts on which it might be helpful to meditate throughout our lives, I would suggest: Dt 1:29-33; 7:7-11; 8:5-10; 11: 10-17; 32:10-11; Is 43:1-7; 49:14-16; 54:5-10; 55; Hos 11:1-9; Ps 103; 139; 145; Lk 7:36-50; 12:22-32; 15:11-32; Jn 3:16-17; 14:14-28; Eph 1:3-14; Jas 1:17-18; 1 Jn 4:9-10.

John Donne beautifully expresses the connection between stability and being captured by God:

> *Take me to you, imprison me, for I,*
> *Except you enthrall me, never shall be free,*
> *Nor ever chaste except you ravish me.*[1]

2. Being grateful for God's gifts, especially for one's calling to serve the poor.

St. Vincent was utterly convinced that we should be grateful for our calling. "Let us give thanks to God for this happy choice!" he cries out on December 6, 1658, during his conference on the end of the Congregation.[2] Through solidarity with the poor we will share their lot, and in doing so, we will also share in the promise of the beatitudes: they are truly happy who are poor in spirit, who hunger and thirst for justice. The Lord blesses not just the poor themselves, but their friends.[3]

Expressing our gratitude to the Lord is the basic meaning of what we do when we celebrate the eucharist. Active participation, with a grateful heart, will both reflect and deepen our dependence on him.

Expressing to others a similar gratitude for our calling will be a sign that we really do believe deeply in the "new order of things," in which the poor are first and in which serving them is a gift that we have received in joyful faith.

One of the practical signs of gratitude for our calling is the willingness to share the gift, by encouraging others to join in this same happy calling. In that light, vocational promotion both expresses and deepens our commitment to serve the poor in the Congregation for the whole of our lives.[4]

---

1. *Holy Sonnets*, V.
2. SV XII, 77.
3. Cf. SV XI, 392: "God loves the poor, and consequently he loves those who love the poor. For when you love someone deeply, you have affection for his friends and his servants."
4. In his later years, as he became more concerned about the survival of the Company, St. Vincent began to take a more active interest in vocations. In 1655, he writes to Etienne Blatiron (SV V, 462-63): "I thank God for the special devotions you have committed yourself to in order to ask God, through blessed St. Joseph, for the spread of the Company. I beg his divine goodness to accept them. For twenty years I never dared to ask for this, thinking that, as the Congregation was his work, care for its conservation and growth should be left only

Another practical sign of gratitude for our calling is encouragement of those struggling with difficulties. Experience says that most, at one time or another, find themselves confused, wandering, uncertain where to turn. Dante, speaking of the "middle years," puts it strikingly:

> *Midway upon the journey of our life*
> *I found myself within a forest dark,*
> *For the straightforward pathway had been lost.*
> *Ah me! how hard a thing it is to say*
> *What was this forest savage, rough, and stern,*
> *Which in the very thought renews the fear.*
> *So bitter is it, death is little more.*[1]

In such times supportive listening and friendship on the part of someone who is grateful for his own calling can be the sustaining force that enables others to persevere. It also can be a source of growth for the listener.

3. Avoiding bitterness, negative criticism

One of the strongest enemies of community is bitterness and negative criticism. They corrode the heart of the individual and eat away at the life of the group. St. Benedict was so aware of this that he prescribed flogging for those who were habitual gripers![2] St. Vincent too recognized it as a plague that the Congregation must avoid contracting.[3]

Right from the start, then, it is important to learn the ways of channeling criticism constructively, of not allowing small issues to become burning ones, of creating the processes for constructive dialogue. More will be said in this regard when discussing the active involvement that contemporary obedience demands of us.

---

to his providence. But from thinking about the recommendation given in the gospel to ask him to send workers into his harvest I have become convinced of the importance and usefulness of this devotion."

1. *The Divine Comedy* I, 1-7.
2. *Rule of Benedict*, ch. 23.
3. SV IX, 75, 122; X, 432-33; XII, 456, 473; cf. *Common Rules of the Daughters of Charity*, 31 (the version used by St. Vincent, as found in the CEME edition: Salamanca, 1989, 124): ". . . above all, they will avoid murmuring about the way the superior or superioress acts, or about the Rules and good customs of the Company, because that kind of murmuring is capable of bringing down a curse from God, both on the person who murmurs and on the one who listens to her eagerly, and even on the whole Company on account of the great scandal it causes."

4. Renewing one's commitment frequently

A good means used by many throughout the history of the Congregation and of other communities is to renew one's vowed commitment frequently. Some choose to do this even daily; others do it on the occasion of significant events or anniversaries.

In renewing their commitment, some simply repeat the vow formula they originally used. Some use their own words. Some use the words of the saints. There are many such prayers or formulas that can help. Some might find themselves attracted, for example, by St. Vincent's prayer:

We are weak, O God,
and capable of giving in at the first assault.
By your pure loving kindness
you have called us;
may your infinite goodness, please,
now help us persevere.
For our part, with your holy grace,
we will try with all our strength
to summon up
all the service and all the faithfulness
that you ask of us.
So give us, O God, give us the grace
to persevere until death.
This is what I ask of you
through the merits of Our Lord Jesus Christ
with confidence that you will remember me.[1]

Others may easily identify with St. Ignatius' renewal of commitment, often recommended by the Church:

Lord Jesus Christ,
take all my freedom,
my memory, my understanding, and my will.
All that I have and cherish
you have given me.
I surrender it all to be guided by your will.
Your grace and your love
are wealth enough for me.
Give me these, Lord Jesus,
and I ask for nothing more.

---

1. SV IX, 360.

2. Chastity

Toward a contemporary understanding[1]

For the modern reader, what St. Vincent says about chastity may seem much too negative, restrictive, outdated. The modern world has a considerably more positive view of relationships between men and women than did the writers of the seventeenth century. We find it unsettling that so much of what St. Vincent writes is couched in precautions and a pessimistic view of human nature.[2]

At the same time we know that chaste celibate living[3] is quite as much a challenge in our day as it was in his, perhaps even more so. Yet, in today's context, we prefer to express that challenge in a more positive way even if, in evaluating things honestly, we must acknowledge that, for varied reasons, we sometimes fail to meet the challenge.

But moving beyond the language and rhetoric characteristic of the seventeenth century, it is important for us to attempt to express the meaning of and the means for living celibate love so that it makes sense for us today.

a. Of course, celibacy, like every way of following Jesus, is all about loving. The "Program for Vincentian Formation in the Major Seminary" puts it this way:

> (We vow) chastity, lived out wholeheartedly in celibacy, which leads
> us to open our hearts more and more to God and to the neighbor,
> without discrimination (CR IV, 1; C 29; 30), and which we receive
> as a gift from God and as a way of following Christ who gave himself
> up for all of us and loved us unreservedly.[4]

Notice the elements in the description: 1) chaste celibate love is a gift from God; 2) this gift calls us to a two-fold response—to allow ourselves to be more and more captured by God and to be more and more immersed in love of the neighbor, without discrimination; 3) the revelation of the gift and the

---

1. For the basic ideas presented in recent Church documents, cf. PC 12; ET 13-15; PO 16; *Sacerdotalis Caelibatus* (June 24, 1967); Canon 599; *Directives on Formation in Religious Institutes* (February 2, 1990) 13.
2. Cf. R. Deville, *op. cit.*, 173ff., on the pessimism that characterized the spirituality of St. Vincent's time.
3. Without delaying here to debate the terminology, I will use the terms "chaste celibate living" and "chaste celibate love" to describe our calling rather than simply "chastity." As is evident to the reader, the latter term is more general and describes the gospel call to all Christians. Nor will I enter here into the much discussed issue of the canonical requirement that all priests in the Latin rite make a commitment to celibacy. The focus in this article is on the vow to live a chaste, celibate life which priests and brothers are called to make freely as members of the Congregation of the Mission.
4. *Vincentiana* 32 (1988) 164 #14c.

paradigm for our response to it are seen in the humanity of Jesus, as he expresses his love for the Father and for us. This description captures many of the essential elements that give flesh and spirit to the celibate commitment.

One might add a fourth element to this description; namely, that chaste celibate love is both a call to and a sign of deep faith and hope in the kingdom.

b. For those who struggle with celibacy, meditation on the humanity of Jesus provides striking encouragement. It reveals that healthy, fruitful celibate living is an existential possibility. Jesus is utterly caught up in the life and work of his Father. At the same time, he loves his brothers and sisters with a warm, outgoing, human love that embraces all. It is he—this celibate— who reveals in his humanity what it means when we say that God is love.[1]

The genuineness of Jesus' relationship with his Father leaps off the pages of the gospels. This is most evident in Luke and John. In Luke, for instance, Jesus turns to the Father again and again in prayer:

3:21 When all the people were baptized, and Jesus was at prayer after likewise being baptized, the skies opened and the Holy Spirit descended on him.

5:16 He often retired to deserted places and prayed.

6:12 Then he went out to the mountain to pray, spending the night in communion with God.

9:18 One day when Jesus was praying in seclusion and his disciples were with him, he put the question to them, "Who do the crowds say that I am?"

9:28 About eight days after saying this he took Peter, John and James, and went up onto a mountain to pray. While he was praying, his face changed in appearance.

10:21 At that moment, Jesus rejoiced in the Holy Spirit and said: "I offer you praise, O Father, Lord of heaven and earth, because you have hidden from the learned and the clever what you have revealed to the merest children."

11:1 One day he was praying in a certain place. When he had finished, one of his disciples asked him, "Lord, teach us to pray, as John taught his disciples."

11:5 He teaches them two parables on prayer.

18:1 He teaches them two further parables on prayer.

22:39 Then he went out and made his way, as was his custom, to the Mount of Olives; the disciples accompanied him. On reaching the place, he said to them: "Pray that you may not be put to the test."

---

1. On a secular level too, some are so caught up in the pursuit of a value that they renounce even marriage in order to focus their energies, their time, their attention on it. Socrates is the classic example. In more recent times, Albert Schweitzer is often cited.

23:34 Jesus said, "Father, forgive them; they do not know what they are doing."

23:46 Jesus uttered a loud cry and said, "Father, into your hands I commend my spirit." After this he died.

At the same time, in Luke's gospel, this great man of prayer is also the Evangelizer of the Poor. He is utterly caught up in proclaiming and witnessing to the good news of his Father's universal love.

Jesus' style of ministry in Luke is the style of the herald (*keryx*) of the ancient world. He announces *kerygma*, good news. "The Spirit of the Lord is upon me," Jesus tells those in the synagogue at Nazareth, "therefore he has anointed me. To preach good news to the poor he has sent me" (Lk 4:18). He moves from town to town in a mobile ministry (Lk 4:43-44). He warns his followers not to get tied down by material needs: "The foxes have dens, the birds of the air have nests, but the Son of Man has nowhere to lay his head" (Lk 9:58). "Sell what you have and give it to the poor. You will have treasure in heaven. Then come follow me" (Lk 18:22). He tells them to be free, detached, able to go wherever the Father calls them. "If anyone comes to me without turning his back on his father and mother, his wife and his children, his brothers and sisters, indeed his very self, he cannot be my follower" (Lk 14:26).[1]

Jesus' celibate life-style frees him for a mobile ministry. In a sense, his celibacy and his ministry interact with one another. Celibacy liberates him to be radical in showing lack of concern about material possessions, house, homeland, wife, or even the offspring that might carry his own life-blood into the future. Because Jesus as a celibate does not root himself in immediately tangible values, he is freer to pursue single-mindedly those which are intangible. He is able to focus his whole life explicitly on his Father and go wherever the Father sends him to proclaim the good news.

c. Following Jesus, the celibate places his stock in a value that is not seen (or at least is seen "only darkly as in a mirror"), the kingdom of God, and in doing so he renounces a value that is quite visible and deeply appreciated by many, marriage. The celibate renounces the prolongation of his life and his gifts in his children, believing that another form of love, which he has freely chosen, will be prolonged in and fruitful for the kingdom of God.

Seen from this point of view, generous celibate love[2] is always a challenge to the honest observer. Because the observer appreciates the value of mar-

---

1. Cf. Mt 19:29; Mk 10:29, where the motivation for renunciation is "for me and for the gospel."
2. Of course, if celibacy is not lived generously, the honest observer may interpret it as being based not on belief in the power of the kingdom of God, but on any number of other motives (the desire for security, comfortable bachelorhood, etc.).

riage, he knows that a genuine celibate is guided by, and trusts deeply in, an unseen light, believing that the kingdom of God is at hand and that the Lord of the kingdom has the power to give him "a hundred times" as many children in the present and unending life in the world to come (cf. Mk 10:28-30).

In this sense, faithful celibacy is intimately related to that radical evangelical poverty of spirit that places all its future in God.

Stealing a phrase from Basil Hume,[1] we may aptly describe the vowed life, and especially celibacy, as a love that is "reckless but disciplined."

It is *reckless*, because the love that is the life of the kingdom of God dares great things. It ventures beyond the securities that most people cling to. It looks on material things not as "my own," but as "ours"; it sees them as ways of sharing God's love with our brothers and sisters. It centers on the Lord as the focus of life and is willing to renounce even wife and children to be with the Lord single-mindedly. It seeks not its own desires or its own will in life, but what the Lord asks as he speaks through the community. It throws in its lot with the poor, the abandoned, the outcasts of society. Only through "reckless" love can a person do these things, a love that is free to abandon human securities and leap into the arms of the Lord.

Yet the great paradox is that this love must also be *disciplined*. Undisciplined love, as Erich Fromm points out,[2] is often mere romance or flirtation. It lacks the qualities that are at the heart of all genuine love: constancy, fidelity, sacrifice. Disciplined love seeks the Lord day after day. It focuses on him, as the psalmist says, in rising up in the morning and in going to bed at night (cf. Ps 92:3). It knows celibacy not only as a joyful, freeing gift, but also as a demanding life-style. It knows poverty not only as generous sharing, but also as personal asceticism. It knows obedience not just as availability to the community and its works, but also as renunciation of a central part of oneself.

e. In that light, let me offer three reflections about this quest for the kingdom of God with a "reckless but disciplined" love.

1) **Freely-giving, mature celibate love is not so much an achieved end as a goal to be striven for.** A vowed commitment, like all commitments, is not a task accomplished once for all; it is a pilgrimage, a journey.

There will be failures on the journey. Just as we can fail in speech, in justice, in charity, so also we can fail in celibate love. It is a serious mistake to think that sexual sins are the gravest of failings. On the contrary, the Lord seems much more understanding of them than he is of pride and injustice.

There is a wonderful story told by the desert fathers:

---

1. Basil Hume, *Searching for God* (London: Hodder and Stoughton, 1977) 49-53.
2. Erich Fromm, *The Art of Loving* (New York, 1956) 108.

A brother questioned an old man, "If it happens that someone gives way to temptation in consequence of some impulse or other, what may befall him through those who are shocked by it?" He replied, "In an Egyptian monastery there was a famous deacon. Now an official, prosecuted by the judge, came to the monastery with his whole family. Driven by the Evil One, the deacon sinned with the man's wife, and he became a cause of scorn to everyone. So he went to an old man among his friends and made the matter known to him. Now the old man had a sort of crypt behind his cell, and the deacon begged him, 'Bury me there alive, and tell no one.' He went into this dark place and did strict penance. Some time later, the river did not flood, and while everyone was saying litanies, it was revealed to one of the saints that the water would not rise unless a certain deacon who was hidden with a certain monk came. On learning this they were filled with astonishment and went to bring the deacon out from the place where he was. And he prayed, and the water rose, and those who before had been shocked were much more edified at his repentance, and they gave glory to God."[1]

2) **Celibacy should be "generative."** The mature celibate must keep his creative powers alive and use them in a publicly identifiable way. Erich Erikson puts it rather starkly:

> *To know that adulthood is generative does not necessarily mean that one must produce children. But it means to know what one does if one does not.*[2]

Since the celibate does not bear children, he must develop an expanded sense of responsibility for life. In this sense, St. Vincent is a wonderful example of celibate love. For him, celibacy does not become an escape from loving; it becomes, rather, a stimulus to love all the more. He promotes life wherever he finds it struggling to survive and grow: in the poor country people, in the clergy called to serve them, in the sick poor, in the foundlings, in the galley slaves, in the Vincentians, in the Daughters of Charity, in the Ladies of Charity, in the wealthy who were searching for a way to use the gifts God had given them. "Love is inventive, even to infinity," he tells the members of his Company.[3]

Such "generativity" calls for a broadening of one's vision, an expansion

---

1. This story, found in the collections of the saying of the desert fathers, is among the selections in Thomas Merton, *Wisdom of the Desert.*
2. E. Erikson, *Dimensions of a New Identity* 123.
3. SV XI,146; cf. also SV IX, 139-40, where St. Vincent tells the Daughters: "O my God! O my God! My Daughters, what a consolation! You are virgins and mothers at the same time. Yes, you are mothers of these poor children. . . ."

of interests, moving beyond oneself and one's present works. It demands a knowledge of one's own gifts and an eagerness to share them.[1]

The more mature the celibate is, the more will he grow in the ability to be intimate without domination or jealousy. His responses will liberate others rather than bind them to himself. His choices will be determined by care for the good of others rather than by preoccupation about others' reaction to himself. He will know how to transcend genital sexuality by finding creative ways of being together and working together with others in the service of the kingdom.

3) **There are varying ages of celibacy.** Each age has its own challenge. When we are young, the challenge is often the physical drive of sex. Later, it is the need for companionship, or intimacy with one other person for whom I am special and who is special to me. Still later, it is the desire for children, for someone to bear my life and my image into the future. And still later, it may be the need for companionship again, for someone whose life I will share and with whom I will find mutual solace in my declining years.

Loneliness enters everyone's life, whether married or celibate. It signals our incompleteness, our need to reach outside ourselves to find fulfillment. A recent survey in the United States indicates more than ninety percent of the population feel loneliness at one time or another, and that twenty-five percent feel severely or painfully lonely at any given time; only one or two percent seem never to be lonely.[2] It is evident, therefore, that from time to time virtually everyone experiences the need for intimacy as a gnawing desire. The celibate must seek to transform such loneliness into a healthy solitude, where he can find his true self, find God, and find the capacity for creative human relationships.[3]

The challenges are always new. They vary from person to person and from one stage of life to another. In each of the "ages of celibacy" there is the tendency to take refuge in immature compensatory measures, rather than face the challenges of creative love. One could compile a long list of immature refuges: vicarious participation in the sexual experiences of others;[4] absorption with cultivating one's own physical appearance; denying or demeaning

---

1. Along similar lines, cf. the Lenten 1990 letter of the Superior General to the members of the Congregation of the Mission: "Celibacy is about life. . . . To be celibate is to transmit that life which has its source in the loving heart of the celibate Christ. . . . The task that we have taken on through our vow of chaste celibacy, is to give life to others and to give it to them more abundantly. The question, then, that we can pose to ourselves at the end of any day is: To whom have I given life today? Whose life have I enriched by prayer, by work, by action, by understanding, by patience, by compassion?"
2. Jeanne George, "Loneliness in the Priesthood," *Human Development* X, 12-15.
3. John Shea, "Intimacy in a Celibate Community," *Human Development* X, 16-20.
4. This is a temptation which is by no means restricted to celibates, as is evidenced by the widespread trade in pornographic literature, films, and video-tapes.

the value of marriage or the pleasure of genital expression; taking refuge in fantasies of sexual gratification and conquest; masturbation; fear of self-disclosure; and protective partnerships.[1]

Toward a contemporary practice

As means for living celibacy healthily today, let me suggest six stabilizing factors that, if present in the life of a celibate, will help him to love faithfully, joyfully, and creatively.[2]

1) Prayer

Karl Rahner puts the matter utterly clearly: "Personal experience of God is the heart of all spirituality."[3]

One of the purposes of the vows is to help us focus explicitly on God. They are meant to facilitate our praying. Likewise, our praying will facilitate living out our commitments. As mentioned above, this is very evident in the life-style of Jesus.

In our Vincentian context, as a concrete means, let me suggest the importance of fidelity to the one hour of personal prayer daily demanded by our Constitutions.[4]

2) "Job Satisfaction"

In a survey of thousands of priests and religious more than a decade ago, those who experienced the greatest peace in living their commitment were those who found "job satisfaction," or joy in their apostolates.[5] If someone is happy in what he is doing, the burdens of commitment will not be so heavy.

Langdon Gilkey once wrote: "Work and life have a strange reciprocal relationship: only if man works can he live, but only if the work he does seems productive and meaningful can he bear the life that his work makes possible."[6]

---

1. These are related to the "particular friendships" referred to by St. Vincent (CR VIII, 2), but different too, in that the latter usually focus on possession and control, while the former may really be a largely unrecognized conspiracy among persons to maintain their isolation from others.
2. Cf. Program #60, for a similar listing.
3. K. Rahner, "The Spirituality of the Church of the Future," in *Theological Investigations* XX, 150.
4. Const. 47.
5. *Readiness for Ministry*, published by The Association of Theological Schools in the U.S. and Canada, Vandalia, Ohio, 1975-76.
6. L. Gilkey, *Shantung Compound* (San Francisco: Harper and Row, 1975) 52.

We cannot "create" happiness; nor is it found by seeking it in itself. It comes in company with other values. In this case, let me suggest that dedicated service to the poor and the clergy can be a source of great joy and satisfaction and can make celibate living much less burdensome.

3) Community and friendship

No man is an island. Besides prayer and work-satisfaction, all of us need human support. "A faithful friend is a secure refuge; whoever has found one has found a treasure," the Book of Sirach tells us (6:14). St. Vincent was quite aware that the community must attempt to provide an atmosphere in which confreres live as "friends who care for one another deeply,"[1] and where they sense that they can grow. This need is similar, if not greater, today and will continue to be so. Karl Rahner speaks of "fraternal community as a real and essential element of the spirituality of tomorrow."[2]

Today too we are aware, in a renewed way, that healthy contact with one's own family and with other friends can be a strengthening, rather than debilitating, force in celibate life. The value of genuine friendship has, of course, perennially been recognized. Cicero sums it up eloquently, reflecting on his relationship with Atticus:

What is more pleasing than to have someone to whom you can express things as openly as to yourself? What savor would success have, if there were not someone to be as happy about it as yourself? Wouldn't it be harder to bear the blows without someone who feels them more keenly than you do?[3]

4) "Honest Talk"

As a help on the journey, it is important to have the courage to speak confidentially about our sexual struggles and failures with a spiritual director or confessor, as with the Lord. Experience teaches that other wayfarers are ready to accompany us on the celibate journey, are very understanding of our weakness, and know the pitfalls along the road.

Unfortunately, the practice of spiritual direction sometimes falls into disuse after ordination or profession of vows.[4] Yet few things are more

1. CR VIII, 2.
2. K. Rahner, "The Spirituality of the Church of the Future," in *Theological Investigations* XX, 150.
3. *On Friendship*, section 6.
4. Cf. SV XIII, 142, where St. Vincent recommends spiritual direction explicitly to those being ordained.

helpful in dealing with intense feelings, concerns, and problems. The struggles we experience in regard to sexuality are often embarrassing, but "honest talk" with a mature director is often the wisest first step in handling them. In the letters quoted in the first part of this article, St. Vincent is very clear about this.[1]

Conversely, problems too long held within us, or dealt with in isolation, often cause enormous personal confusion and eventually explode. Anyone without a soul friend, the ancient Celtic saying goes, is a body without a head.

5) Personal Discipline and Prudence in Relationships

In my earlier chapter on the five characteristic virtues, I made a number of concrete suggestions in regard to personal discipline.[2] Discipline helps in achieving many of the values we commit ourselves to: prayer, work, study, a simple-style, and celibacy too. In fact, few values are achieved without it. In that sense, it is an incarnational reflection of grace, or of the constancy of God's love.

Though we might be put off by the negativity of what St. Vincent writes concerning the need for caution in relationships with women, there is a perennial wisdom at its core which can be applied in a context where relationships between men and women are seen much more positively: not just *any* time, or place, or circumstance is appropriate for relationships; this is true not just for celibates, but for married and single people as well. While today we recognize that it is not possible to draw up a precise casuistry in this regard, a celibate must be mature enough to know his own limitations and disciplined enough to live within their bounds. Common sense says, on the one hand, that it is normal to have friends who are women; it says, on the other hand, that our relationship with them should be guided by prudent norms. One of these is that physical expressions of affection, especially when people are alone, often tend in the direction of greater attraction and greater involvement. Surely that is the wisdom in St. Vincent's concern about a confrere's being "solus cum sola, loco et tempore indebitis."[3]

Discipline in the use of alcohol is also a helpful factor not just in regard to one's physical health, but also in regard to celibate life. Many who have

---

1. He writes to Jeanne Lepeintre on February 23, 1650 (SV III, 614): "Spiritual direction is very useful. It is a source of advice when in difficulties, of help when discouraged, of safety when tempted, and of strength when overwhelmed. Finally, it is a source of benefit and consolation when the director is really charitable, prudent and experienced." St. Vincent often spoke on the need for spiritual direction. Cf. XII, 451-85; XIII, 142.
2. Cf. p. 65-67.
3. CR IV, 2.

made commitments to celibacy and to marriage testify that sexual problems began or evolved when their inhibitions had been lowered by drinking too much.

6) A Balanced Life-Style[1]

While the Lord calls us to be servants, he wants us to rest too (cf. Ps 127:2; Ex 20:8ff). As a matter of fact, he commands us to rest![2] He calls us to recognize our limitedness as creatures and to know that not only does he work through us, but that he also works without us.

People who are worn out and discouraged experience problems with celibacy readily. Difficulties that at other times they might more easily handle become insurmountable problems. It is important (not just for celibacy, but for overall health as well) to listen to one's body, to know when tiredness is sapping one's strength, to recognize the signs of irritability or anger or poor judgment that signal exhaustion. St. Vincent often warned St. Louise to beware of "indiscreet zeal."[3]

3. Poverty

Toward a contemporary understanding[4]

a. In the conciliar and post-conciliar Church, perhaps no call has resounded more clearly or more frequently than the call to evangelical poverty. In response to Christ, the Church wants to be the Church of the poor. The same holds true for the Congregation. The Superior General's Lenten letter of 1989 puts it forcefully: "The Church is the Church of the poor, and the poor are its preferential option. The option for the poor is fundamental to the Congregation; it inspired the birth of the Company and will be the source of its present and future vitality as well. If the Church cannot be conceived of

---

1. For a very good treatment of this subject, as well as for much practical wisdom in regard to each of the vows, cf. Wilkie Au, *By Way of the Heart. Toward a Holistic Spirituality* (New York, 1989) 41ff.
2. There are many interesting studies on the theology of rest. Cf. K. Rahner, "Sunday, the Day of the Lord," in *Theological Investigations* VII, 205-10; J. Huizinga, *Homo Ludens, a Study of the Play Element in Culture* (London: Paladin, 1970); J. Pieper, *Leisure, the Basis of Culture*; H. Rahner, *Man at Play*.
3. SV I, 96: "It is a ruse of the devil by which he deceives good souls. . . ." Cf. CR XII, 11; also SV I, 84; II, 140; X, 671.
4. For many of the basic ideas present in contemporary Church documents, cf. PC 13; ET 16-22; PO 17; Canon 600; Directives on Formation in Religious Institutes (February 2, 1990) 14.

without reference to the poor (like the mission of Jesus and the whole gospel message), the same must be said for the Congregation, because the reason for our existence in the Church is to continue the mission of Christ the Evangelizer of the Poor."[1]

The "Program for Vincentian Formation in the Major Seminary," following the example of St. Vincent, immediately appeals to the witness of Christ, when it speaks about poverty. It states that we vow:

... poverty, which identifies us with Christ, poor and humble, frees us to share the life of the poor and employ what we are and what we have in their service, regarding them as our portion and our material goods as their patrimony.[2]

b. But though the call to evangelical poverty, both in the Church and in the Congregation, has been clear, many have experienced that finding the concrete ways to respond to that call has been difficult, even sometimes frustrating. Let me suggest that one of the reasons for this difficulty, besides cultural factors and the temptations of the "affluent society," is the complexity of the concept of "evangelical poverty." The gospels, the conciliar documents, and our own Constitutions emphasize various facets of poverty. While this is a sign of the concept's richness, it also makes it difficult to speak about evangelical poverty univocally. Note, for example, the following aspects of poverty, as found in our own Constitutions:

1) *Poverty of spirit*[3] lies at the core of the gospel. It is the first of the beatitudes and the foundation of New Testament spirituality. It is the attitude of the poor of Israel, of whom Mary is the first. It is the humility that characterizes those who know their complete dependence on God, who long for him, who listen eagerly for his word. It is a recognition of our own creatureliness. It sees all life as gift and turns to God, the giver of all good gifts, with gratitude. It is a detachment that never mistakes the gift for the Giver. It is being free not to have. On the deepest level, it is a renunciation of all forms of wealth, including power and prestige. It is an acknowledgment of our own sinfulness and our need for ongoing conversion and redemption. It is the pre-requisite for being evangelized. In the minister, it is indispensable, if he is really to be evangelized by the poor.

2) *Poverty in fact*,[4] experience teaches, is closely related to poverty of spirit. To grow in genuine poverty of spirit, the follower of Jesus must develop a special attitude toward material goods, seeing them, in a sense, as

---

1. *Vincentiana*, 33 (1989) 6.
2. Program, 14c; cf. CR III, 1; C 12, 3°; 31.
3. Cf. C 31; 34; also Mt 5:3.
4. Cf. C 33; 12, 3°; also Lk 9:58.

an extension of his own body. His material goods, like his body, must be ways in which he reaches out to the neighbor. They must be signs of his love.[1] If given away, they will be a way of giving his person and God's love that is within him. If stored up, they will be a way of isolating him from the world and of cutting him off from the kingdom of God. For this reason the wisdom of religious communities has always included recommendations toward simplicity of life, especially as it touches on things like our houses, rooms, clothing, food, travel, and entertainment.

3) *Sharing with the poor*[2] is one of the central New Testament themes. "Sell what you have and give it to the poor," Jesus says in the synoptic gospels (cf. Mt 19:21; Mk 10:21; Lk 18:22). Even more strikingly, in Matthew's twenty-fifth chapter he proclaims that the central criterion for judgment is whether or not we have actually shared with the poor when they were hungry, thirsty, homeless, naked, imprisoned (Mt 25:31-46). Genuine solidarity with the poor through extending God's love to them concretely is the sign of genuine Christian faith and love (cf. Jas 2:14-26; 1 Jn 3:17). Of course, this is very much a part of the Vincentian tradition. The Church and the Congregation today call us to share not only our material goods with the poor, but also to share in some way in their condition, to work within the world of the poor, to confront injustice with them, to labor not just for them but with them, "so that the poor person is an agent, and not simply an object, of evangelization."[3]

4) *Community of goods*[4] receives great emphasis in the Book of the Acts as Luke paints the picture of the ideal Christian community. The members of the community, like Jesus and the apostles (cf. Jn 13:29), hold all things in common. Luke describes a vibrant, caring community where there is no longer anyone in need, because those who had more sold their goods, so that the needs of others could be satisfied. Reflection on poverty as "community of goods" has concrete ramifications like budgeting and accountability for the use of goods.

5) *The common law of labor*[5] binds members of communities just as it binds the poor. In fact, Jesus repeatedly attempts to instill into his followers, especially the leaders of the community, a servant's attitude (cf. Jn 13:12-16; Lk 22:25-27; Mt 25-28; Mk 10:42-45; Phil 2:5). Their labor will be one of the signs of their love. In religious communities, such love has often been

---

1. Cf. *Evangelica Testificatio* 17, henceforth ET.
2. Cf. C 33; 35, 152; also Mt 19:21.
3. "The Visitors in Service of the Mission" (Rome, January 25, 1990) 16; cf. Const. 12; LA 4 and 11.
4. Cf. C 32; 25, 4°; 148; 149; 154; also Acts 2:42; 4:34.
5. Cf. C 32; also 2 Thes 3:12.

shown through tireless work in schools, hospitals, orphanages, as well as in preaching, visiting the sick, and ministering to the various other needs of the poor.

6) The *evangelical witness*[1] given by those living simply in solidarity with the poor has received great stress in our own documents and in those of the universal Church.[2] In fact, especially at a time when society places so much emphasis on material prosperity, it is striking when someone renounces his possessions in order to serve the poor and remains content with little by way of material goods. This is one of the signs of the kingdom that continues to fascinate the honest observer.

7) *Asking for permission*[3] has traditionally been a part of the vow of poverty, though one might also situate it on the boundary between poverty and obedience. This tradition, found in all religious communities, has two roots: a) the recognition that we form a community of goods, and that consequently we should submit important decisions about the use of those goods to the community itself (through its superiors); b) the recognition that we are sinful and tend always to want more, and that consequently we should submit our own judgment to that of the community when there might be the danger of self-deception.

8) Very much a part of our own tradition has been *the tension between absolute poverty and what is needed for the apostolate.*[4] This is especially evident today. To labor well for the poor, communities often needs cars, computers, sophisticated X-ray or CAT-scan machines, etc. St. Vincent recognized in his day that, as an apostolic community, the Congregation must use contemporary means for serving the poor and training the clergy. But of course, this does create a tension. It demands prudent judgment, capable of distinguishing what will really promote the apostolate goals of the Congregation from what is merely a comfortable luxury.

In analogous fashion, there is also at times a tension between poverty and community needs. Today, for example, giving candidates the education they will need for the future is, in some countries, a very costly matter; but it may be a quite necessary expense. Likewise, providing for the future of the elderly by appropriate health care, or social security, or medical insurance may also be a costly, but indispensable undertaking.

I mention the eight facets of evangelical poverty described above in order to illustrate the complexity as well as the richness of what is involved in our

---

1. Cf. C 31; 33; also 2 Cor 8:8.
2. Cf. ET 18-19.
3. Cf. C 34; 35; 155.
4. CR IV, 2; cf. C 33; 35; 148; 154.

vowed commitment. The tendency in times of complexity is to seek solutions that are over-simplified; someone might, for example, declare, without nuance, that "poverty of spirit," or "asking permission," or "sharing" is what we really have to concentrate on. It is imperative to resist this temptation. Rather, in order to do justice to the gospels, contemporary Church documents and our Constitutions, we must find ways of living out evangelical poverty on a variety of levels. An honest examination of conscience should take into account all of the factors mentioned above.

The matter becomes even more complex when one attempts to address the question of communal poverty, as St. Vincent did, and the proper use of the goods of the Congregation as a whole, of the provinces, or of the local houses for the promotion of justice and charity.

c. Let me suggest that two concepts, much emphasized in contemporary Church documents, may be helpful in sharpening our focus in regard to evangelical poverty: 1) solidarity, and 2) communion.

Many of St. Vincent's principal concerns in regard to the vow of poverty might be grouped under the concept of solidarity: solidarity with the poor and solidarity with our brothers in the Congregation in the service of the poor.[1] Solidarity with the poor demands that we share with them what we have, that we stand with them in resisting and working to change the unjust social structures that oppress them,[2] that we ourselves experience some of the sting of poverty. "Only one who is poor of heart, who strives to follow the poor Christ, can be the source of an authentic solidarity and a true detachment," state the recent Directives on Formation.[3] Solidarity with our brothers in community demands that we make decisions together about the use of our community's resources, and that together as a team, each fulfilling his own task, we observe the common law of labor in the service of the poor.

Communion draws us "to be of one mind and one heart" and "to possess all things in common." *Sollicitudo Rei Socialis*,[4] in a statement reminiscent of St. Vincent, points out that its model is the Trinity. Communion is the soul of the Church's vocation as a sacrament. And like the life of the Trinity, as well as the life that bound together Jesus and the first disciples, it is utterly outgoing. It embraces the most abandoned with a preferential love.[5] In this sense, genuine communion with God is the soul of poverty of spirit, and genuine communion with the poor is the ground for our sharing their want and their pain. The Congregation's witness in the world depends on both.

---

1. Cf. John Paul II, *Sollicitudo rei socialis* 26, 38-40.

2. *Ibid.* 36-37.

3. *Directives on Formation in Religious Institutes* (February 2, 1990) 14.

4. Cf. #40.

5. *Ibid.* 42.

Toward a contemporary practice

Let me offer, at least as a starting point for concretizing the practice of poverty today, a series of imperatives based on our Vincentian tradition:

1) Be poor in spirit. Recognize your need for God's word and his saving love. Listen humbly and well to all. Allow yourself to be evangelized by the poor.

2) Learn to see all life as a gift. Share that gift generously with others: your time, your service, your goods. Develop detachment by giving freely.

3) Be poor in fact. Accept some of the privations that poor people experience, especially as regards lodging, food, and material comforts.

4) Eat what is set before you. Do not complain about food. Drink moderately.

5) Develop a simple life-style. Let your room, your clothing, your entertainment be quite modest.

6) Give generously to the poor from your personal belongings; encourage the Company to do likewise from its corporate holdings. Resist the temptation to "capitalize" your money.

7) Often examine conscientiously how you live and work, whether you use the Company's own goods frequently on yourself or whether you share them generously with others, especially the poor.

8) Hand over your earnings to the community joyfully, without holding back, so that a true community of goods may be established.

9) Ask the required permissions humbly, recognizing in yourself the tendency toward acquisitiveness that lies within all of us. But make your life of poverty more than simply the obtaining of permissions to own things.

10) Be sparing in the things you acquire. Practice a consumer asceticism. Resist pressure from the media to "have to have."

11) Be willing to labor hard, both in the daily chores of community life and in the labors of the apostolate. Develop a "servant's attitude."

I must here add a final brief word on a communal poverty, a topic that demands greater attention than it can be given here. Two of the foremost twentieth-century theologians have made strikingly contrasting statements about communal poverty. Yet different as their statements are, both shed considerable light on the question.

Yves Congar once wrote that communities cannot, and even must not, practice the radical evangelical poverty that individuals are called to.[1] As

---

1. Y. Congar, "The Church and Poverty," in *Unam Sanctam* 57 (Paris: Cerf, 1965) 155.

mentioned above, they have a responsibility to prepare their young members—a rather expensive task today. They also have an obligation to take good care of their elderly, something that in many countries now involves enormous expense. Surely communities must meet these and other obligations generously and responsibly.

On the other hand, Karl Rahner once wrote that it is impossible to be poor in a rich community.[1] When communities have too much money, they often wind up spending it for their own comfort. What to others might seem a luxury becomes to such communities an affordable necessity. Within such a setting, it is difficult for even the sincerest member to live a life of evangelical poverty.

Conscious of this, a number of house plans and provincial plans today determine that a certain proportion of the community's income (sometimes ten percent) will be given to the poor.

On a provincial level, even more can be done. Concretely, let me suggest that, within provinces, policies be established for the responsible use of the Congregation's assets. Reasonable estimates must certainly be made about how much money a province needs for carrying out its works, educating its present and future members, and caring for the sick and elderly. But when those reasonable sums have been set aside and wisely invested, our norms should determine how the rest of our assets can be turned to the best advantage of the poor. One might apply to such monies the famous axiom of St. Ambrose: "You are not making a gift to the poor person. You are handing over to him what is his."[2]

4. Obedience

Toward a contemporary understanding[3]

The problematic

a. In some ways obedience is the most difficult of all the vows to write about.[4]

1. Cf. K. Rahner, "The Theology of Poverty," in *Theological Investigations* VIII, 172.
2. *De Nabuthe*, c. 12, n. 53 (PL 14, 747). Cf. *Populorum Progressio* 23.
3. For many of the basic ideas presented in contemporary Church documents, cf. *Perfectae Caritatis* 14 (henceforth PC); ET 23-28; *Presbyterorum Ordinis* 15 (henceforth PO); Canon 601; Directives on Formation in Religious Institutes (February 2, 1990) 15.
4. I must, in order to keep this article within reasonable size-limits, restrict the discussion here to obedience in community life. There is, naturally, much that could also be said (as a

Each of the vows focuses on the following of Jesus and finds its foundation in the gospels. The call to evangelical poverty in the New Testament is strikingly clear, as mentioned above. Likewise it is evident that some are called to a celibate life "for the sake of the kingdom of God." And finally, the scriptures state unambiguously that Jesus always seeks and does the will of his Father (cf. Jn 4:34; 5:30), and calls his followers to do the same.

But there is a giant step from seeking and doing the will of God to carrying out the will of another human person and regarding that as the will of God.[1] The step would be easier to take, though it would still have to be nuanced carefully, if Jesus had invested religious superiors with special authority and promised to be with them guiding their actions, as he does with the leaders of the Church. But nothing in the New Testament indicates that such is the case with the heads of religious communities. Such institutions receive no special guarantees from the gospels, other than those given to all believers in Jesus. Those who enter communities, moreover, do so by their own free choice. They are also free not to enter. How can they freely bind themselves by vow to obey someone who, like themselves, is quite limited in his insight into God's will?

b. The problem is further complicated because, among the explanations of obedience offered in the course of history, there have been many distortions. The modern reader may find himself quite uncomfortable, for example, when he hears St. Vincent telling the confreres to obey with "a certain blind obedience."[2] While it is clear that St. Vincent himself was aware of the need for using a qualifier ("a *certain* blind obedience"), still, especially since the experience of Nazism, we are quite aware that the phrase may do more harm than good.

Other distortions are less obvious. Sometimes, for instance, the language used in describing obedience reveals that the paradigm proposed is the parent-child relationship. But this cannot be a sound basis for religious obedience. The parent-child relationship rests on the presumption that the parent is mature and that the child is immature; one would hope that this is not the case in religious life. Moreover, as a child reaches adulthood, his obligation to obedience gives way to other duties based on adult-to-adult standards, but in religious life the obligation to obedience remains throughout life. Even in those cases in religious life where greater maturity on the part

---

complement to this discussion) about the role of authority in religious life, but that must await another occasion.
1. Below, I will offer a brief outline of some of the factors essential for discernment of God's will in community. The role of superiors is one part (even if an important one), among many others, in this overall process.
2. CR V, 2.

of the superior is to be presumed, as when a "master" trains a "novice," the goal of the process is its own gradual disappearance, with the learner, one hopes, becoming in his turn a master.

Surely it is also a mistake to employ a paradigm that thinks of superiors as more learned or more gifted morally or spiritually than those living in the communities they govern. History teaches the lesson that this is often not the case. Even if it should be true in a particular case, it is not an adequate basis for making a vow covering all cases.

Nor, in attempting to explain obedience, can one simply say: "It is good to give up my will," or even, "It is good to give up my own will as Jesus did." Why is it good? To whom does one give it up? One cannot renounce responsibility for one's own actions so easily. We are, after all, morally responsible for our own acts and must seek always to direct them toward what is good.[1]

It is also a mistake, in explaining obedience, to reduce the authority of superiors to mere "regulation of traffic" or "maintenance of good order." Even if at times the role of the superior has been exaggerated, the tradition of communities, as well our contemporary documents, sees them as key figures in the discernment process (or, to use the contemporary term, as primary animators). Our own recent document on the role of the Visitor, for example, describes his mission in terms that go far beyond mere traffic regulation: "The Visitor's mission is to be *in service of the unity of the province as it seeks and does the will of the Father*, who is the salvation of all in Jesus Christ."[2] In other words, he is to be a primary animator in the province. Our Constitutions speak even more concretely about superiors' relationship with the community, calling confreres to "try by light of faith to obey decisions of superiors even when they consider their own views better."[3]

The root question, in light of all this, remains: how do we know that in doing the will of another we are doing the Father's will?

The context for obedience[4]

c. In attacking this question, it is important to note from the start that the

---

1. Cf. G. Aschenbrenner, "A Diocesan Priest's Obedience," in *Human Development* 10 (1989) 33.
2. "The Visitors in Service of the Mission," January 25, 1990, in *Vincentiana* 33 (1990), para. 6.
3. Const. 37, 2.
4. For an excellent treatment of obedience and discernment, cf. Wilkie Au, *By Way of the Heart* (New York, 1989) 114-135.

over-arching goal of the virtue and vow of obedience—creating an environment in which a community and the individuals within it are eagerly seeking to do the Father's will—is much more demanding than individual acts of obedience that might be carried out merely by reason of the vow. Johannes Metz writes: "Obedience as an evangelical virtue is the radical and uncalculated surrender of one's life to God the Father who raises up and liberates."[1] The acts that concretize the living out of the vow should flow out of this virtue of obedience; at the same time, they should nourish the virtue.

But in the concrete that might not always be the case. In some contexts, superiors and other members of the community, satisfied with their own lights, may actually make meager efforts at listening carefully to others and discerning the will of God. This, unfortunately will distort the process of obedience right from the start.

Sound obedience, in service of the mission, finds its deepest roots within the larger context of a community that is sincerely seeking the will of God. Such a community has a number of readily discernible characteristics:

1. it loves God as a Father and thirsts to do his will;
2. it reads and reflects communally on the word of God;
3. it prays together;
4. its members listen to one another with deep respect;
5. they listen to the directives of Church (e.g., conciliar documents, encyclicals, the law of the Church, etc.) and of their own larger community (e.g., its Constitutions and Statutes, Provincial Norms, etc.);
6. they discern the signs of the times communally, especially the cries of the poor;
7. they engage in ongoing formation, listening to teachers from both inside and outside the community.

Without such characteristics a community is likely to be blind. Its superiors and its other members will be prone to seek their own will, their own goals, their own security, their own comfort, rather than what the Lord is asking. Their decisions, while perhaps juridically correct, will scarcely be an authentic reflection of the gospel.

Bernard Lonergan speaks scathingly of such a situation:[2] "The fruit of unauthenticity is decline. Unauthentic subjects get themselves unauthentic authorities. Unauthentic authorities favor some groups over others. Favoritism breeds suspicion . . ."

---

1. J. Metz, *Followers of Christ* (Ramsey: Paulist, 1978).
2. Bernard Lonergan, "Dialectic of Authority," published in *A Third Collection* (New York: Paulist, 1985) 9.

Given the context described above, contemporary theology seeks to articulate a reasonable basis for the vow of obedience as a function of our commitment to community.

Obedience as a function of community[1]

d. To attempt to clarify the matter, let me suggest a series of propositions.

1. When a person enters a community, he binds himself to a definite way of life within the Church. Such a life involves a mission.[2] It focuses on service of God and his people, and involves prayer, life together, and service in community with others, within the framework of the Church. In joining our own Congregation, we bind ourselves to live in this particular "apostolic society." We explicitly state that we vow to dedicate our whole lives to the service of the poor *in the Congregation of the Mission.*

2. All such freely-chosen societies in the Church need, and in fact have always evolved, decision-making processes. The processes vary considerably historically. Sometimes they are monarchical (though always with some limitations), as was the case with many "superior-subject" relationships until fairly recent times. Sometimes they are democratic, as with the General Assemblies of many religious congregations. Today, they are usually a mixture of checks and balances.

3. In committing ourselves to *community*, we commit ourselves to its *decisions.* If we really wish to belong to a given community, with its given apostolic ends, approved by the Church as part of her mission, we commit ourselves to live by that community's decisions. In this sense, looking back over history, obedience was originally included in the "one vow" of joining a religious community; only gradually did it come to be explicitated as a separate vow.

4. It may vary considerably over the course of time *how* authority is chosen in a given community and *how* it will reach its decisions.[3]

---

1. For a very good treatment of this subject, with abundant citations from St. Vincent, cf. Giuseppe Guerra, "Autorità e obbedienza nella Chiesa," *Annali della Missione* LXXXVI (1979) 55-69.

2. The connection between obedience and mission is emphasized in the recent *Directives on Formation*, 15: "Whether one has authority in an institute or not, one cannot either command or obey without reference to mission."

3. Occasionally, some make the error of thinking that obedience is more perfect if the system imposing it is monarchical. This is not necessarily true at all. Obedience, like most Christian values, is not restricted to any particular type of governmental system or cultural context (though the temptation for those living in a particular culture may be to think that it is). Democratic processes can result in decisions that are quite binding and that make difficult

Sometimes today those in authority are appointed (e.g., most bishops today); sometimes they are elected (e.g., the pope, many provincials today, many bishops in the past). Sometimes they reach their decisions monarchically, sometimes collegially, sometimes democratically.

5. But in any event, in all historical periods, with their varying cultural contexts, *some* form of obedience will be necessary if religious communities are to exist. Even in a very democratic structure, obedience is very much a reality (sometimes a stinging one) since those who might favor a minority position must ultimately obey the decision enacted by the majority.

6. Within this context, in which obedience is seen as a function of membership in community, it may be helpful to offer a few reflections on the *scope* of obedience, a topic often reflected on in foundational writings of communities.

- If they are to be truly binding, all norms and commands must be related to the end and various goals of the particular apostolic society. More traditionally, this has been stated in terms like these: "We owe obedience to superiors . . . *according to the Constitutions and Statutes.*"[1] In other words, the power of superiors is limited; it does not go beyond the framework set up within the society. This is, in modern times, a touchy area, since the line between one's "private life" and one's "community life" is not always an easy one to discern, as our Constitutions acknowledge.[2]

- All norms and the commands of superiors, to be binding, must also be just. More traditionally, this has been stated in terms like these: "One must obey in all matters where sin is not evident."[3] In other words, the superior's commands cannot run against the moral law, as interpreted by a well-informed and well-advised conscience. Another way of saying this is that laws or commands must be reasonable. This is evident, since a law is, by definition, a dictate of reason. Consequently, it should be noted that superiors cannot ask foolish things of others just to test their mettle.

---

demands. At a General Assembly, for example, a democratic system is used for electing a Superior General and for composing Constitutions and Statutes. Afterwards, all the members are then bound to obey the General and live by the Constitutions. The asceticism of obedience makes demands not just on those who voted for another candidate or for a different version of the Constitutions (and *against* the accepted version), but for everyone, since faithful observance and generous response to leadership demands follow-through and constancy.

1. Cf. C 38.
2. Cf. C 22.
3. Cf. CR V, 2.

But, on the other hand, it should also be noted that in many contexts, as is evident in the "information society" described in Part II, there are often a number of reasonable ways to proceed (not just the one I might think is best) and the superior must eventually choose only one (and perhaps not the one that I might favor), which the community is then called to abide by.

7. Beyond the obligation to obey the commands of superiors, obedience involves a commitment to follow a way of life, as described in a Rule or a Constitution. In fact, since explicit commands are rather rare, the obedience involved in living out the Constitutions and other norms is much more a regular part of life than the obedience involved in responding to the commands of superiors.

Today we would say that such norms demand "substantial observance." Implied in this is the conviction that if one generously observes the substance of the law (allowing for reasonable exceptions) he will grow in the values the law attempts to foster in individuals (e.g., that they become prayerful apostolic men) and will contribute toward the common good of the community (e.g., that, filled with such men, the community will give vital witness to the good news among the poor).

8. Since obedience is a radical commitment to community and its decision-making processes, a person deepens his "belonging" to community to the extent that he lives out its decisions and he "withdraws from" community to the extent that he fails to abide by them. These decisions are manifested on a variety of levels: Constitutions, Statutes, various ordinances and provincial norms, provincial and local plans, the decisions of various superiors, etc.

Notice that such an understanding of obedience (as an intrinsic element in committing oneself to community) coincides with St. Vincent's desire to have vows *for the sake of the mission.* It is because we want to belong to an apostolic, missionary community in the service of the poor that we make a vow of obedience.[1]

Toward a contemporary practice

The key to obedience, like the key to genuine community, is listening. The word *obedience* (*ob* thoroughly + *audire* to hear) itself makes this clear. How central this is not only to the vow of obedience, but to all New Testament

---

1. Cf. "The Visitors in Service of the Mission," *Vincentiana* XXXIV (1990), 43, para. 19: "Everything said in Rio about the Visitor's role as animator has our mission as a final reference point, but our mission as carried out in a communal way."

spirituality is one of the main themes of Luke's gospel. It is impossible to treat this theme at length here because of limitations of space, but the reader may wish to meditate on the many passages in which Luke reiterates the importance of listening: e.g., 8:19-21; 10:38-42; 11:27-28; cf. also 1:26f.; 1:39f.; 2:16f.; 2:36f.; 2:41f.). One of the great challenges in community today is the designing of processes in which listening is highlighted. A community will do the will of God only to the extent that its members, and particularly its leaders, can really hear what God is saying.

Because of this, it is evident, especially today, that obedience is binding not just on "subjects," but also on "superiors." The demands on both are great. Together, both are called to seek the will of God. In order to do this, both must listen well.[1]

Today we place great emphasis on the need to listen *in community*. As Bernard Lonergan often pointed out: "Community means people with a common field of experience, with a common or at least complementary way of understanding people and things, with common judgments and common aims. Without a common field of experience people are out of touch. Without a common way of understanding, they will misunderstand one another, grow suspicious, distrustful, hostile, violent. Without common judgments they will live in different worlds, and without common aims they will work at cross-purposes."[2] Our Constitutions and Statutes, recognizing the importance of the input of all the confreres in decisions affecting their lives, sometimes use the phrase "the superior with the community" to describe the process for arriving at decisions.[3] They also demand frequent meetings of all the confreres of the houses, who will act like a council for superiors.[4] To the extent that confreres participate actively in the meetings, consultations, and dialogue that are part of our present-day structures, they will be *subjects* of decision-making and obedience rather than merely its objects.

The law, now as in the past, allows the superior, except in a relatively small number of cases, to act contrary to the advice of his councillors. In allowing this freedom, the law reflects the conviction that truth does not always reside with the majority. Religious obedience is not merely vote-counting; it involves dialogue and listening on the part of all. But, while it is clearly legal for a superior to go against the advice of his council, it is also

---

1. ET 25, puts it this way: "Far from being in opposition to one another, authority and individual liberty go together in the fulfillment of God's will, which is sought fraternally through a trustful dialogue between the superior and his brother, in the case of a personal situation, or through a general agreement regarding what concerns the whole community."
2. *Ibid.*, 5-6.
3. Cf. C 129, 2; S 78, 4°.
4. S 79, 3.

clear, from a moral point of view, that a superior who frequently does so runs the risk of grave imprudence.[1]

Given this background, it is evident that obedience today is a much broader and much more demanding concept than simply obeying the commands of superiors. Within this framework, let me outline some contemporary means for practicing obedience as we vow it today. Our Constitutions and Statutes and other present-day sources tell us that, for a Vincentian, contemporary obedience involves:

1. entering into open and responsible dialogue[2]
2. listening carefully to the opinions of others, to data about the signs of the times, to the call of the gospels, to directives and lines of action of the Congregation[3]
3. taking active part in consultations[4]
4. assisting at and contributing to meetings[5]
5. contributing actively to the formulation of the local community plan, and faithfully carrying it out[6]
6. taking initiative[7]
7. obeying decisions of superiors in the light of faith even though we may think our own opinion better[8]
8. striving to achieve unity in mind, heart and action[9]
9. being concretely available to go to any part of the world[10]

Let me conclude these reflections on the four Vincentian vows by renewing my appeal for reactions and further efforts toward concretization on the part of others. I trust that through dialogue we can deepen our understanding of and commitment to the vowed life. In doing so, we will better accomplish the missionary goals given us by St. Vincent.

The vows play an extremely important role in the life of the Congregation, not just as history but as prophecy. If fully lived out, they make the gospel come alive. They witness to the presence of the kingdom of God, "already"

---

1. K. Rahner, "A Distinction: Legal and Moral Norms," in *Studies in Modern Theology* (London: Burns and Oates, 1965) 394-400.
2. C 24, 2°; 37; 46; 97.
3. C 2.
4. C 96; cf. S 68, 69, and many other places where confreres are asked to respond to consultation. Cf. also C 134, on the house council.
5. C 96; 97; 136; S 79, 3.
6. C 27; S 16.
7. Cf. C 129, which states that the Congregation "forms itself in the local communities" and that the superior "with the community" promotes the ministries of the house and is concerned for the growth and activities of each.
8. C 37, 2.
9. C 24.
10. C 12, 5°.

in our midst but "not yet" here in its fullness. In a changing world, a changing Church, and a changing Congregation, they have a vital function. As he envisions the Church of the future, Karl Rahner writes:

> *The spirituality of the future will be a spirituality of the Sermon on the Mount and of the evangelical counsels, continually involved in renewing its protest against the idols of wealth, pleasure and power.*[1]

1. K. Rahner, "The Spirituality of the Church of the Future" 145.

Chapter IV

COMMUNITY LIVING AND THE COMMUNITY PLAN

*Be united with one another, and God will bless
you. But let it be by the charity of Jesus Christ,
for any union which is not sealed by the blood
of Our Savior cannot perdure. It is therefore in
Jesus Christ, by Jesus Christ, and for Jesus
Christ that you ought to be united with one
another. The Spirit of Jesus Christ is a spirit of
union and of peace. How can you attract people
to Christ if you are not united with one another
and with him?*

St. Vincent de Paul
(Abelly, book II, c. 1, 145)

Jesus lived in community with his apostles. They shared their lives
intimately with each other. They prayed together often. Jesus instilled in his
followers the great vision that his Father had given him of a kingdom of
justice, love and peace which they could begin to experience and work
toward even now. He asked them to preach that kingdom to others, but first
to make it real in their own lives. They shared a common purse, from which
they paid for food and lodging. When they returned home from preaching,
they spent time together resting and enjoying each other's company.

The early Christians were so struck by this example that they idealized
about what community should be like:

*The community of believers were of one heart and one mind. None
of them ever claimed anything as his own; rather, everything was
held in common.* (Acts 4:32)

In this chapter I will attempt to describe what goes into building up a
Christian community and then offer a detailed analysis of one of the means
the Constitutions of the Vincentians and the Daughters of Charity suggest
for renewing our efforts at re-creating the reality that Jesus and his apostles
lived in common.

SOME FOUNDATIONAL NOTIONS ON COMMUNITY

Below, I will briefly outline four key concepts in regard to community.

1. Community is a gift of God; it is at the same time a human creation. Both of these assertions have deep New Testament roots. ✓

Community as God's gift

When speaking of community, St. Vincent goes quickly to its theological roots. He sees its foundations in the mysteries of the Trinity and the Incarnation. In this light he recommends devotion to these two mysteries to his followers.[1] The Vincentian Constitutions see these mysteries as the foundation of the Church, and, within the Church, of the Congregation of the Mission.[2]

All true community finds its source in God. Jesus' union with his Father is the paradigm for the intimate bonds that link his followers together in the Spirit. It was reflection on Jesus' mission to draw all together in the Father's love that led the Christian community to reflect more deeply on God's inner Trinitarian life.

Since its source is in God, all community is ultimately gift. It is possible only through God's love as it works in us through Christ:

> *I do not pray for them alone, I pray also for those who will believe in me through their word, that all may be one as you, Father, are in me, and I in you; I pray that they may be in us, that the world may believe that you sent me.* (Jn 17:20-21)

Dietrich Bonhoeffer puts the God-givenness of community quite strikingly:

> *It is true, of course, that what is an unspeakable gift of God for the lonely individual is easily disregarded and trodden under foot by those who have the gift every day. It is easily forgotten that the fellowship of Christian brethren is a gift of grace, a gift of the kingdom of God and any day may be taken from us, that the time that still separates us from utter loneliness may be brief indeed. Therefore, let him who until now has had the privilege of living a common Christian life with other Christians praise God's grace from the bottom of his heart. Let him thank God on his knees and declare: It is grace, nothing but grace, that we are allowed to live in community with Christian brethren.*[3]

---

1. CR X, 2.
2. C 20.
3. D. Bonhoeffer, *Life Together* (London, 1954) 9-10.

But he also speaks of the need for us to respond to God's gift: "In a Christian community everything depends on whether each individual is an indispensable link in a chain. Only when even the smallest link is securely interlocked is the chain unbreakable."[1]

All God's gifts demand a human response; community, therefore, is not only God's work but our work too.

Community as a human creation

Though St. Vincent often reflected on community's roots in God, even more often he wrote and spoke about the human means for building and nourishing it. The Rules he gave to his communities,[2] the letters he wrote,[3] and the conferences he gave[4] got down to very concrete norms for living together.

The Vincentian Constitutions likewise emphasize both the vertical and horizontal dimensions of community's coming-to-be. "The Church finds the ultimate source of its life and action in the Trinity. The Congregation, within the Church, does the same," article 20 states. At the same time, article 129 §1 states: "The Congregation forms itself particularly in the individual local communities."

So while community is God's gift, we are his instruments in creating it. Without us it cannot come into being. St. Paul emphasizes the human effort that goes into building community:

> I plead with you then, as a prisoner for the Lord, to live a life worthy
> of the calling you have received, with perfect humility, meekness,
> and patience, bearing with one another lovingly. Make every effort
> to preserve the unity which has the Spirit as its origin and peace as
> its binding force. (Eph 4:1-3)

2. True community does not stifle diversity; on the contrary, it sees itself as enriched by the varied gifts of different members.

The New Testament abounds in imagery when it describes community. It is a body with all its varied members. It is a vine with many branches. It is a pilgrim people with diverse gifts. The images focus on unity in diversity, as in Paul's first letter to the Corinthians:

> Through the Spirit one received faith; by the same Spirit another is

---

1. *Ibid.* 72.
2. Cf. CR VIII, 1.
3. Cf. SV VIII, 100, where St. Vincent consoles Antoine Durand, superior at Agde: "I feel for you in the pain that you suffer."
4. Many of his conferences, even on seemingly different topics, are actually on means for living well together; cf. SV XII, 244ff.

*given the gift of healing, and still another miraculous powers.
Prophecy is given to one; to another power to distinguish one spirit
from another. One receives the gift of tongue, another that of
interpreting the tongues. But it is one and the same Spirit who
produces all these gifts, distributing them to each as he wills. The
body is one and has many members, but all the members, many
though they are, are one body; and so it is with Christ. . . . Now the
body is not one member, it is many. If the foot should say, "Because
I am not a hand I do not belong to the body," would it then no longer
belong to the body? If the ear should say, "Because I am not an eye
I do not belong to the body," would it then no longer belong to the
body? If the body were all eye, what would happen to our hearing?
If it were all ear, what would happen to our smelling? As it is, God
has set each member of the body in the place he wanted it to be. If
all the members were alike, where would the body be?* (1 Cor
12:9-22)

The Vincentian Constitutions emphasize the same idea: "The initiatives
of members should be evaluated in the light of the purpose and spirit of the
Congregation. In this way the individuality and charisms of each member
come together to foster community and make the mission effective" (C 22).
Another paragraph states: ". . . the evangelization of the poor . . . gives to all
our work a unity that does not stifle diverse talents and gifts but directs them
to the service of the mission" (C 25, 2°).

Diversity is not the enemy of community. It is part of its richness. The
Rule for a New Brother puts this rather beautifully:

> *Be thankful for the variety of gifts and difference of personality.
> When you put your own potential and insights at the service of your
> community your unity will grow stronger and richer, and together
> you will create that spaciousness which finds room for everyone.*[1]

3. True community is not simply physical or functional presence. It is being *with* and *for* the other person.

People can have physical presence to one another as strangers in an
elevator. They can have functional presence to each other if they work
together on an assembly line in a factory. But in neither of these instances is
there true community. True community is being with and for the other. It is
personal concern and care (even if often within the context of a project).

The Vincentian Constitutions strongly emphasize the personal dimension
of community. They call the members of the Congregation to renew the

---

1. *Rule for a New Brother* (London, 1973), ch. 3.

principal elements of their way of living and acting, first of all by "following Christ the Evangelizer as a community, which generates in us special bonds of love and affection; in this spirit we should, 'like good friends' (CR VIII, 2) join reverence for one another with genuine esteem" (C 25, 1°). In this, of course, they echo the New Testament:

> This is how all will know you for my disciples: Your love for one another. (Jn 13:35)

4. True community is not a static reality. It is always being created.

This characteristic of community is stated quite explicitly in the Vincentian Constitutions (C 25): "The Community is continually responsible for its own development. . . . " This means that true community involves initiative, to get things going. It involves forgiveness, to heal what has gone wrong. It involves ongoing formation. It is always being created. We make a grave mistake when we think of community as an *abstract* reality (as if a "community" can exist statically and we can simply move into it). True community is concrete, dynamic. It consists of real people who work at building it up rather than the imaginary people we dream of. Dietrich Bonhoeffer once wrote: "The person who loves his dream of community more than the real community itself destroys community."[1]

> You form a building which rises on the foundation of the apostles and prophets, with Christ Jesus himself as the capstone. Through him the whole structure is fitted together and takes shape as a holy temple in the Lord; in him you are being built into this temple, to become a dwelling place for God in the Spirit. (Eph 2:20-22)

LEVELS OF COMMUNITY

From what has been stated above, we should not be surprised that community is very imperfect at times. If community really is something we must work toward, then it can never be captured once for all. We must always be striving to create it. Sometimes there will be high points, sometimes lows. We will have better community in one house than in another. We will have better community in some matters than in others. I say this, because as Bernard Lonergan points out, community demands union on many levels, some of which may be better realized than others. Lonergan speaks of four levels at which the bonds of community are forged.[2]

1. Bonhoeffer, *op. cit.*, 15.
2. Bernard Lonergan. *A Third Collection* (Mahwah, N.J., 1985) 5-6.

1. Common experience

Common experience lays the groundwork for community. It is what initial and ongoing formation programs try to create. It involves understanding a common heritage, sharing in common traditions, learning common ideas through our studies, participating in common symbolic acts, being immersed in and reflecting together on common works, living a common life-style.

When people first come together they often do not have much common experience. So it must be worked at. A confrere who has spent his whole life on the missions may find that he has little in common with a confrere who has spent much of his life teaching theology. When they enter a local community together, they will have to work hard at making community real.

2. Common understanding

Common understanding means that when we *say* the same things we *mean* the same things. Take sin, for example. For one person it may mean breaking a law. For another it may mean breaking a relationship. For one person God may be a judge. For another he may be a loving father. For still a third, he may be the sum total of world forces. One person may view the Church as a predominantly hierarchical institution where new directions come mainly from above. Another may see the Church as the people of God where new ideas bubble up from below. For these people to come to a common understanding (and they will never perfectly achieve that goal) will demand much dialogue.

3. Common judgment

This means that we come to agree, as a community, on certain ideas. "We hold these truths"; e.g., those contained in a constitution. Vincentians as a body hold that the end of the Congregation of the Mission is to follow Christ the Evangelizer of the poor. When a new member comes to join the community, he must assimilate the basic common judgments that are *foundational* to the community. There will also be many other more concrete, practical common judgments that particular local communities come to agree on; e.g., that they will celebrate the eucharist together each day; that the best time for this is at 7:00; that their life-style should be simple, and at the same time warm and family-like; that they will work both in a parish and in a school;

that in their school, the policy regarding admissions will be . . . , etc. Reaching common judgments demands meetings, a decision-making process, a willingness to compromise, and respect for differing opinions. Even in the best of times, however, disagreements over judgments, and especially over means, will remain. The body of *foundational* common judgments will not be excessively detailed, nor very large; moreover, while the most basic truths will remain stable, their interpretation will never be static.

4. Common action

A community must act together on the judgments which it has made. The members must work with one another in such a way that they feel co-responsibility. If the community merely has common experiences, common understanding, and common judgments, but its members do not carry them into action, then it is not a true community. It lacks follow-through. It is in agreement ideologically, but not committed in actuality.

The commitment to obedience, which has played a part in all Christian communities, comes into play on this level. Members of a community must be resolved that after consultation and dialogue, they will work together in acting on common judgments, even if some (or even many) continue to hold dissenting views.[1] Obedient, loving dissent is a healthy reality in community and can provide the basis for ongoing dialogue. As Socrates pointed out, dissent is a function of loyalty to the group, even if at times it may create some discomfort for the members.

In summary then, true community involves all four levels: common experience, common understanding, common judgment and common action. Sometimes these will be more fully realized; at other times, less fully.

THE COMMUNITY PLAN

The new Constitutions of both the Vincentians[2] and the Daughters of Charity[3] offer a practical means for renewal in community life, the local community plan. I want to suggest that this can be a particularly effective means for renewal if those in a given community enter into it as a *covenant*. If through dialogue based on common experience, we can come to greater

---

1. Cf. C 37, 2.
2. C 27; cf. S 16.
3. *Données à Dieu pour le service des Pauvres* 3.46; cf. S 57.

common understanding and formulate common judgments, we can covenant before God and with one another that we will live out in common action what we have agreed on. The community plan will serve as the written statement of that covenant.

I am convinced that we are still struggling to find adequate concrete means for renewing community life and have not yet been fully successful in the quest. But much of the problem is quite understandable. We have passed from a long period in which the structures of community living were universally legislated. Thirty years ago, for example, if a Visitor went to Rome or to Rio he would find that, even though the Vincentians there spoke a different language, the basic forms of community life were quite familiar. The community rose at 5 A.M., went to morning prayer and meditated for an hour. Then there were probably private Masses, breakfast, and time for the apostolate. At midday there was a particular examen, followed by lunch. In the evening, the community prayed vespers and perhaps anticipated matins before supper. Later it joined in a common night prayer, after which the grand silence began.

Today most of these universally legislated structures have disappeared. Within the rather general framework of Constitutions, Statutes, and Provincial Norms, each local community is asked to agree on the structures that will concretize the various aspects of its life: how will we carry out our specifically Vincentian mission in this house, how will we share life with one another, when and how will we pray together, how often will we meet for dialogue as part of the decision-making process, what meals and other "family" times together will we commit ourselves to, etc.? In place of universally legislated structures, we are called to create *covenanted* structures. The questions above set the stage for some of the decisions that form the covenant.

It is evident that covenanting demands great creativity and responsibility from the members of the local community. No longer are there many universally legislated structures that bind us from without; it is up to us to create structures that bind us from within. And, of course, covenanting implies that, having made common decisions and created local structures, we will abide by them.

In the paragraphs that follow I offer an outline of what the Vincentian Constitutions and Statutes say about the local community plan and some models of what such plans might look like.

a. The statements of the Vincentian Constitutions and Statutes concerning the community plan

1. The basic legislation for the local community plan is found in C 27 and S 16.

C 27 *Each community should work at developing a community plan, according to the Constitutions, Statutes, and the Provincial Norms. We should use this plan as a means of directing our life and work, of fulfilling the recommendations we receive, and of examining periodically our life and activities.*

S 16 *The Community Plan which each community draws up for itself as far as possible at the beginning of its work year, should include: apostolic activity, prayer, the use of goods, Christian witness where we work, ongoing formation, times for group reflection, necessary time for relaxation and study, and an order of the day. All these should be revised periodically.*

2. Several other paragraphs in the Constitutions and Statutes refer explicitly to the local Community Plan:

C 32 §1	Confreres' work responsibilities
S 19	Acts of piety
S 69, 5°;78 ,4°	Approval by the Provincial
S 78, 4°	Formulation by the local superior together with the community

3. Still other paragraphs provide relevant background for better understanding the plan:

C 23	Proper autonomy of local community
C 25	Need for local community to renew itself
C 129	The Congregation forms itself particularly in individual local communities
S 79 §3	Frequent meetings should be held

4. Many other paragraphs suggest matter that might aptly be included in a community plan: S 3; C 17; S 9 §2; C 24 2°; S 18, S 37 §1; C 96; C 149; C 152; etc.

5. In addition, a number of matters treated in the Provincial Norms might properly be included among items to be treated in a community plan.

6. Some other paragraphs in the Constitutions and Statutes refer directly or allude to a Provincial Plan, which might be generated from the local community plans: S 37 §2; S 69 1°; etc.

b. Models of what a community plan might look like

Three models for a community plan follow. These can be used freely, of course. There could be other models. A community plan could, for example, simply follow the outline of the Lines of Action of the General Assembly and agree on concrete steps for carrying them out.

MODEL I

(I would recommend that this model be used by community houses that are beginning the planning process. While taxing, it has the value of helping the local community come into fuller contact with the Constitutions and Statutes and can draw it into reflective discussion of what they demand of us.)

COMMUNITY PLAN OF THE VINCENTIANS
AT

_____

I APOSTOLIC ACTIVITY (S 3, S 9 §2, S 16, C 17, C 23, C 24 2°,C 25, C 96, C 129).

This section might treat the apostolic priorities of the house.

II PRAYER (S 16, S 19, C 25)

This section might treat our daily exercises of prayer, the weekly service of the word, periodic times of reflection, the annual retreat, etc.

III COMMUNITY LIFE (C 23, C, 24 2°, C 25, C 129)

This section might treat the means that the local community chooses for fostering its life together (perhaps these are already treated in other sections of the plan).

IV CHRISTIAN WITNESS IN THE PLACE WHERE WE WORK (S 16, C 20, C 24, C 33, C 44-45, C 49, S 36, S 100).

This section might treat those aspects of our lives that the local community plan sees as its most important witness in its place of work.

V ORGANIZATION (S 16, S 78 4°, S 79 §1 §3, C 24 2°, C 96, C 134 §2)

This section might treat the organizational structure of the local community (e.g., how often it meets, how decisions are made, etc.).

VI ONGOING FORMATION (S 16)

This section might treat the means the local community will take for its ongoing formation (e.g., attendance at workshops, study, meetings and discussions in the house, retreats, guest speakers, etc.).

VII   PROMOTING VOCATIONS (S 36, S 37 §1)
      This section might treat the plan of the local house for fostering vocations (how will the local community find young people who will carry on this apostolate in the future).
VIII RECREATION (S 16)
      This section might treat daily common recreation, the need for periodic time off (balancing work and leisure), annual vacation time, etc.
IX   USE OF MATERIAL GOODS (S 16, C 25, C 33, S 18, C 149, C 152)
      This section might treat how the local community plans to use its material goods, how it will seek to live simply, how it makes decisions in regard to spending money or using its resources, etc.
X   ORDER OF DAY (S 16)
      This section will give the order of day.
XI   EVALUATION AND REVISION OF PLAN (S 16, S 78 4°)
      This section might treat how, when, and by whom the plan is evaluated and periodically revised.

MODEL II

(This model presumes that the local community has already worked out many of the issues involved in the first model. It helps it to situate itself within a larger context, articulate its special Vincentian mission, and covenant some goals for the coming year.)

I   DESCRIPTION OF THE CONCRETE SITUATION
      This section would describe the concrete situation where the confreres of the house minister (e.g., the number and type of people in the parish or school; the resources available; the needs of the people; etc.)
II   MISSION STATEMENT
      In this section, the confreres of the house would formulate a statement describing the specifically Vincentian mission which they carry out.
III   COVENANT FOR THE COMING YEAR
      This section might treat any number of the matters listed in the first model above.

MODEL III

(This model aims at situating the house within the present context and plan of the province and at developing goals in that light. It also assigns specific responsibility and provides for periodic evaluation.)

I   REFLECTION ON THE PRESENT STATE OF THE PROVINCE AND HOUSE

After prayerful reflection on the Constitutions and Statutes, the Lines of Action, and the Provincial Plan, the members of the house might in this section describe what they see as their principal concerns as a house.

II SPECIFIC GOALS FOR THE YEAR AHEAD

In this section a limited number of goals will be formulated and agreed on (e.g., carrying out a home visitation in the entire parish; meeting every Thursday at 4 P.M., followed by evening prayer and supper together; organizing a day of recollection together four times during the coming year; agreeing on a book to be read and discussed once every two months, as a form of ongoing formation; making some systematic contact with young people in the parish or school with a view toward vocational promotion; etc.). Specific responsibility for reaching the goals would be assigned to various individuals or groups, as well as a time-frame.

III EVALUATION

A method for periodic evaluation of progress toward the goals would be stated here.

PART II

Christ is the Rule of the Mission. It is he who speaks, and it is up to us to be attentive to his words.

SV XII, 130

THE WAY OF ST. VINCENT
A RULE FOR SERVANTS OF THE POOR

There is no better way to assure our eternal happiness than to live and die in the service of the poor within the arms of providence and in a real renunciation of ourselves by following Jesus Christ.

SV III, 392

I offer this small work primarily to those who are preparing for life-long commitment in the Congregation of the Mission. But I hope that it will also be of service to many others—especially to the Daughters of Charity and to the hundreds of thousands of lay men and women who have already dedicated their lives in varying ways to following Christ as the Evangelizer of the Poor.

I intend this work as a word of encouragement and of direction, accompanied by the sense of awe that you feel as you stand before the gift of God calling you to be a servant of the poor. I address it directly in the second person singular to each of the candidates whom I have so often spoken to as he came forward for admission into St. Vincent's Company. I trust that the women who read this Rule, envisioning their own contexts, will freely substitute the word "sister" for "brother."

To paraphrase St. Vincent—there is nothing new in this work. It simply describes a way of following Christ. But I assure you that if you walk in this way, if you breathe deeply of St. Vincent's spirit, you will find profound joy, because you will be embodying, like him, the spirit of Jesus whom the Father sent to preach the good news to the poor.

My brother, you come to community freely. If you wish to commit yourself to it for life, seek to understand the spirit of St. Vincent de Paul. Try to live by it.

The call you are responding to is a great one. It is a gift from God. Be very happy then, my brother, and very grateful, that God has led you to a company that shares in the mission of his Son. Listen to St. Vincent's words:

> To make God known to the poor; to announce Jesus Christ to them; to tell them that the kingdom of heaven is at hand! But that we should be called to be associated with, and to share in, the works of the Son of God surpasses our understanding. What! to render ourselves—I do not dare say it—so great, so sublime is it to preach the gospel to the poor, for it is above all else the office of the Son of God, and we are applied to it as instruments by which the Son of God continues to do from heaven what he once did on earth. Great reason have we, my brothers, to praise God and to thank him unceasingly for this grace![1]

Know that, before you commit yourself to the community, you are always free to depart. God offers many ways to men and women. St. Vincent's is not the only one. Unless you are firmly resolved to live in it and have a deep trust that God can make you holy through it, do not enter St. Vincent's Company. The decision to enter is a grave one. Stand before it with great honesty, humility and courage. Decide to enter only if you can do so with great freedom and with trust that God who begins a good work in you can bring it to completion.

But if you should commit yourself to St. Vincent's Company, know that you are committing your whole life. When at some future time—as inevitably happens—you are tempted to go back on that commitment, picture to yourself, as St. Vincent said, countless people with outstretched arms calling you.[2] It is to God, to the poor, and to us your brothers, servants of the poor, that you give your life. If you make that commitment, be faithful to it.

---

1. SV XII, 80.
2. SV I, 252.

CHAPTER I - THE PURPOSE OF THE CONGREGATION

My brother, as you enter St. Vincent's Company, seek to understand its purpose well and to make it your own—to follow Christ the Evangelizer of the Poor. Ponder its meaning. Notice that the purpose of the Congregation does not lie merely in works, like preaching missions or teaching in seminaries, important as these may be. Rather, it is a way of following Christ, a specific way. St. Vincent calls you to focus on Jesus as the Evangelizer of the Poor. This is how he saw him:

> In the eyes of the gentiles he passed for a fool. To the Jews he was a stumbling block. But with all that, he described himself as the Evangelizer of the Poor.[1]

Strive, with your brothers, to realize the purpose of the Congregation in the three ways that flow from our heritage.

1) As St. Vincent's follower, make every effort to put on the spirit of Christ himself,[2] the Evangelizer of the Poor, in order that you may grow in genuine holiness.

2) Then preach the gospel to the poor. This is your pre-eminent work. Listen well, my brother, to the eloquent words of St. Vincent:

> Our inheritance, gentlemen and my brothers, is the poor, the poor; **pauperibus evangelizare misit me.** What happiness, gentlemen, what happiness! To do what our Lord came from heaven to earth to do, and by means of which we too shall go from earth to heaven, to continue the work of God . . . .[3]

3) And assist others, both clergy and lay, in their formation as bearers of good news to the poor. Struck by the need for priests and longing for the reform of the clergy, St. Vincent called his Company to labor for the formation of the clergy. He thought so highly of this work that he could cry out:

> To make good priests is the greatest achievement in the world: it is impossible to conceive anything greater or more important. To devote oneself to making good priests and to cooperate to this end—is to fulfill the very task of Jesus Christ. Our Divine Lord, during his life on earth, seems to have taken it as his very special work to train twelve good priests, his apostles; with this end in view, he designed to stay with them some years to instruct and train them for this sacred ministry.[4]

---

1. SV X, 32.
2. CR I, 3.
3. SV XII, 4.
4. St. Vincent frequently returns to the importance of the work for the clergy. Cf. CR XI, 12; SV XII, 84-85.

Contemplate the Christ of St. Vincent, who comes to preach good news to the poor and to form followers to continue this ministry. Learn to know this Christ and to love him deeply. Share his sensitivity toward the poor. Join with him in his labor to form priests and other ministers. Feel the compassion that throbbed in his heart as he reached out to those who were wandering and aimless like sheep without a shepherd.

Come forward to be a priest or brother in the Congregation of the Mission only if you are firmly committed to walk in his footsteps.

CHAPTER II - THE PLACE OF THE GOSPELS

Listen carefully, my brother, to St. Vincent's striking belief in the power of the gospels:

> *Each one must strive, above all else, to ground himself in this truth: the teaching of Christ can never deceive, while that of the world is always false, since Christ himself declares that the latter is like a house built upon sand, whereas he compares his own to a building founded upon solid rock. For this reason the Congregation shall always make claim to act according to the maxims of Christ, never according to those of the world.*[1]

With these words St. Vincent opens the Common Rules. He was most conscious that the members of his Company should be men of the gospels.

To preach the *gospel* to the poor is to be your mission, my brother. In order to grow in knowledge and love of the gospels, you shall read prayerfully each day, as St. Vincent asked his Company, a portion of the New Testament.

But your preaching is to be in "word and work," St. Vincent says. Your love must be both "affective and effective." So, with the contemporary Church, be very conscious that "action on behalf of justice and participation in the transformation of the world are integral elements in the preaching of the gospel."[2] The words of good news that you proclaim will be credible only to the extent that they are accompanied by works of justice, of love, and of peace.[3]

As a preacher of the good news, the first service that you owe God and your brothers and sisters is to listen. Love of God begins with hearing his word and believing in his love for us: "The marvelous thing is not so much that we love God, but that God first loved us" (1 Jn 4:10). So also your love for the neighbor will begin with listening to him.

Learn, then, to be a *good* listener. Allow yourself to be evangelized by others—by your brothers in community, by those you work with, and especially by the poor. You must first hear the good news before you can preach it.

If you listen well, the word of God will enter your life in strikingly diverse ways, always with a view toward your conversion and growth. Sometimes it will come as food (Ps 19:11) to strengthen you and build you up. Sometimes it will be refreshing water (Is 55:10) to quench your thirst on the journey. But at other times God's word may jolt you like a hammer that shatters a rock

---

1. CR II, 1.
2. Synod of Bishops, 1971, *Justice in the World*, in *AAS* LXIII (1971) 924.
3. Cf. SV VII, 98; VII, 620. In these texts he speaks of the importance of the works of justice.

(Jer 23:29), breaking in on your too-settled ways or your hardness of heart. It may also strike you like a sword (Heb 4:12) to pierce your resistance. Listen to it attentively.

Each morning he awakes me to hear
* to listen like a disciple.*
The Lord Yahweh has opened my ear.

Is 50:4-5

CHAPTER III - SERVICE OF THE POOR

My brother, listen to these memorable words:

Let us love God, my brothers, let us love God, but let it be with the strength of our arms and the sweat of our brow. For it often happens that the various affective acts of the love of God and the interior motions of a humble heart—even if they are good and desirable— are nonetheless suspect if they do not result in effective love. Our Lord himself says: "In this is my Father glorified: that you bring forth very much fruit."[1]

You are a servant of the poor. That is your vocation. Remember both terms of your title: you are a *servant*, and a servant of the *poor*.

Jesus loved the poor deeply. He came to serve them, not to be served. "Let him who would be first among you," Jesus told his followers, "be the least of all and the servant of all." As one who walks in Jesus' footsteps, be content to be a *servant*. Have no proud ambitions. Seek little for yourself. Let your needs be few. Be grateful to God for the little you have and ask for little beyond his service. Know, my brother, that as a servant you will have to work hard. That is the lot of servants and that is what God calls you to commit yourself to. Be generous with your time. Regard yourself as being at the beck and call of "your lords and masters."[2] It is to this that you commit yourself by your first vow.

You are the servant of the *poor*, so love the poor dearly, my brother. Pour out that love day after day. Realize beforehand, however, that your love will often be disappointed. You will meet frustrations in preaching or teaching or laboring for the poor. They will sometimes, as St. Vincent warned his followers, despise you the bread that you give them. But persevere, my brother, with a love that manifests joy and enthusiasm and generosity. If you can do this, you will be sharing fully in Jesus' ministry. Faithful to your vow, you will be dedicating your whole life to the poor in his Company.

But in your ministry, as St. Vincent says, first do and then teach. As a follower of Christ, the Evangelizer of the Poor, your proclamation of the good news will resound in the hearts of your people especially when you give vibrant witness:

1) through the language of works:[3] performing the works of justice and mercy which are a sign that the kingdom of God is really alive among us: feeding the hungry, giving drink to the thirsty, helping to find the causes of their hunger and thirst and the ways of alleviating it;

---

1. SV XI, 40.
2. Cf. SV IX, 119; X, 332.
3. Cf. SV II, 4.

2) through the language of words: announcing with deep conviction the Lord's presence, his love, his offer of forgiveness and acceptance to all;

3) through the language of relationships: being *with* the poor, working *with* them, forming a community that shows the Lord's love for all.

CHAPTER IV - CELIBACY

Read carefully, my brother, the following statements from the Constitutions in regard to celibacy:

> *Imitating Christ in his limitless love for all, we embrace, by vow, perfect chastity in the form of celibacy for the sake of the kingdom of heaven. We accept it as a gift given us by the personal and infinite goodness of God.*[1]

> *In this way we open our hearts more widely to God and neighbor, and our whole way of acting becomes a joyous expression of the love between Christ and the Church which will be fully manifested in the age to come.*[2]

> *Intimate union with Christ, true fraternal communion, zeal in the apostolate, and asceticism supported by the experience of the Church will enable our chastity to grow strong. Through a continual and mature response to the Lord's call, it is a living source of spiritual fecundity in the world and it also contributes greatly to the attainment of human maturity.*[3]

If you choose to enter St. Vincent's Company, my brother, freely choose to live as a celibate. Christ chose a celibate life-style for carrying out his mission and made it clear that, in his footsteps, others are called to be celibate "for the sake of the kingdom" (Mt 19:12), "for my sake and for the gospel" (Mk 10:29), to care for "the affairs of the Lord" (1 Cor 7:32). Celibacy stands as a sign of your faith in values which transcend sexual union. It is a sign of your dedication to a full-time project of prayer, apostolic labor, and missionary mobility in the service of the kingdom of God. As a celibate, you show your love for God and your brothers and sisters by making yourself available to serve them single-mindedly. You show your enthusiasm for the gospel and for the kingdom of God by making them the explicit focus of your life, even to the extent of renouncing the positive value of marriage.

But for celibacy to be a vital sign to others, your life, like Christ's, must be filled with prayer[4] and with joyful, generous service (cf. Mk 10:43-45; Jn 13:4-15; Pt 4:7-8). Strengthened by the community, you must lose your life in the service of others, and in losing it truly gain it. You must not be *self*-conscious about your own fulfillment, but *other*-conscious in complete dedication to God and your brothers and sisters.

---

1. C 29 §1.
2. C 29 §2.
3. C 30.
4. Cf., to cite just a few instances, Lk 5:16; 6:12; 9:18; 9:28; 11:1; 22:39.

Yet like all God's gifts, celibacy entails your own responsibility too. Experience teaches this: you will live joyfully as a celibate only if certain values enrich your life and nourish your love; especially

1) daily prayer
2) generous apostolic service
3) deep human relationships both within and outside the community
4) prudence in these relationships
5) balance and discipline in your life-style
6) honest self-presentation in spiritual direction.

The challenge of celibate living is not easy. But the responsibility, while yours, is not yours alone. The Lord who calls you is faithful.

CHAPTER V - POVERTY

As a member of St. Vincent's Company, my brother, you will vow to live simply. Your vow is a profession to be poor both in spirit and in fact, both individually and communally. While your work, St. Vincent says, will not permit you to practice absolute poverty, you must as far as possible strive to imitate Jesus' poverty.[1]

Poverty must be conspicuous in your life in the community. St. Vincent warned his Company that it would cease to exist when it ceased to be poor. He was deeply convinced that we need to be poor if we are to serve the poor.[2] He told the community that poverty would be its defense and support,[3] that it was of the highest importance that we profess it all times and in all places,[4] that without it we would not be credible as servants of the poor.

These thoughts of St. Vincent are echoed strikingly in the contemporary Church:[5] the Church must be poor with the poor by sharing with them in their need.

To be practical in your efforts to be at one with the poor, my brother, take to heart the simple directives that follow. They will be very demanding if you apply them concretely. But Jesus assures you that the poor will be happy.

1. Strive to be poor in spirit and in fact, both individually and communally.

2. Often examine conscientiously how you live and work, whether you use the Company's own goods mostly on yourself or whether you share them generously with others, especially the poor.

3. Make your life of poverty more than simply the obtaining of permission to own things; rather, be sparing in the things you acquire.

4. Be willing to labor hard, both in the daily chores of community life and in the labors of the apostolate.

5. Accept some of the privations that poor people experience, especially as regards food and material comforts.

6. Give generously to the poor from your personal belongings; encourage the Company to do likewise from its corporate holdings.

7. Hand over your earnings to the community so that a true community of goods may be established.

---

1. CR III, 2.
2. CR III, 1.
3. Cf. SV XI, 232f.
4. Cf. SV XII, 403f.
5. Cf. PC 12-13.

CHAPTER VI - OBEDIENCE

"I am a child of obedience," St. Vincent says.[1] He proposes the following of Christ as the basis for our living this virtue:

The first reason we have for giving ourselves to God that he may grant us this virtue of obedience is . . . the example which the Son of God gave us, and which he lived out during his whole life, which was nothing but a web of obedience.[2]

Community demands common judgments and common action. It inevitably involves decisions with which some will not agree. As you come to community, know, and weigh carefully, that you are committing yourself to carry out at least some directives with which you will not agree. This is a difficult human undertaking. Do not accept this burden unless you are firmly committed to living under obedience for the sake of the community. Ponder well the words of our new Constitutions:

To participate in this mystery of the obedient Christ requires us all to seek, as a community, the will of the Father. We do this through mutual sharing of experience, open and responsible dialogue in which differences of age and outlook interact, so that common directions may surface and develop, and lead to making decisions.

Mindful of the words of St. Vincent, and in a spirit of co-responsibility, members should strive to obey superiors as promptly, joyfully and perseveringly as they can. They should try by the light of faith to obey decisions of superiors even when they consider their own views better.[3]

As you commit yourself to obedience, strive to make your own the dispositions and even many of the practices that St. Vincent proposed in the Common Rules:

In order that the Congregation may advance more easily and rapidly in this virtue, it shall do all in its power to see that the pious custom of neither asking for nor refusing anything shall always be practiced among us. Nevertheless, when anyone discovers that something is either harmful to him or necessary for him, he shall examine the matter before the Lord, and decide whether he ought to manifest it to the superior or not.[4]

No one, having received a refusal from one superior, shall approach

---

1. SV I, 511.
2. SV XII, 426.
3. C 37.
4. CR V, 4.

another superior regarding the same matter without making known to him the previous refusal and the reason for it.[1]

Our own sick shall be persuaded that they are confined to bed in the infirmary not only to be cared for and cured by medical help, but also to teach, as from a pulpit, at least by their example, the Christian virtues, especially patience and conformity to the will of God. . . . Since, among the other virtues demanded of the sick, obedience is very necessary, all shall show it with exactitude not only to their spiritual but also to their medical physicians, to the infirmarian and others assigned to take care of them.[2]

Faithful to St. Vincent's spirit, my brother, seek to respond faithfully to the modern-day demands that obedience may make of you:

1. Study our Constitutions well. Seek too to understand the spirit of the Rules that St. Vincent left the Company. Meditate on both these sources, so that they shape your life and vision.

2. Give generously of your time by taking part in our contemporary decision-making processes (e.g., meetings, questionnaires, letters of consultation).

3. Carry out the decisions of superiors, joyfully if possible, even at times when you might disagree with them.

4. Be ready to respond to the needs of the community and God's people, particularly in accepting assignments.

5. Be faithful to the order of day that has been worked out, after consultation, in your house; in particular, be faithful to the times established for daily prayer and the eucharist.

---

1. CR V, 7.
2. CR VI, 3.

CHAPTER VII - COMMUNITY

My brother, St. Vincent did not set out alone in the service of the poor. He formed a Company with common ideals. Reflect for a moment on St. Vincent's vision of the community.

He saw it as a Company whose whole life would revolve around the good news: it was to preach the gospel to the poor that he knew God had sent it. He saw the Company as outward-oriented, as embarking on a mission. He saw it as a group of men who would be deeply convinced that Jesus had become one of us, that he had formed warm human bonds with his followers, that he had died abandoned, but lives on, reunited with us as Risen Lord. He saw the community as living by Jesus' spirit, as walking now in the footsteps of Christ. He envisioned it as poor, as celibate for Jesus' sake, as obedient, and as a servant of the poor.

Meditate, my brother, on the simple New Testament axioms which St. Vincent proposed for our up-building as a community:

> Acts of charity toward the neighbor ought to be practiced constantly by us, such as: 1) to do to others that which we would justly wish them to do to us; 2) to agree with others and to approve of everything of which the Lord would approve; 3) to bear with one another without complaint; 4) to weep with those who weep; 5) to rejoice with those who rejoice; 6) to show respect for one another; 7) to be sincerely kind and obliging to others; 8) finally, to become all things to all men that we may gain all for Christ.[1]

Seek to avoid those things which are the enemies of community. Avoid the jealousies which St. Paul so often speaks of. Avoid the griping that can be so often divisive. Avoid especially speaking of others' faults. You will very much hurt others individually, and the Company as a whole, if you allow yourself to fall into these failings. Speak words that build up the community rather than tear it down. When criticism is necessary, speak simply, but in such a way that your love for your brothers shines through.

If you cannot find peace with the community as it is or with the people who make it up, then do not enter it; otherwise you would be entering on a way that would lead to great unhappiness. But if you can find basic peace even with this very imperfect Company and its very imperfect members, then enter freely, knowing that though life together will make many demands, it will also bring many joys and the communal support of living with those who sincerely pursue the gospels.

As St. Vincent recognized, fidelity to some basic evangelical imperatives

---

1. CR II, 12.

will help you enormously in living happily in an apostolic community. Note well the list of axioms he offers you above. Meditate on them often and put them into practice.

CHAPTER VIII - SPIRITUAL EXERCISES

Listen, my brother, to what St. Vincent says about spiritual exercises: *Christ our Lord and his disciples had their spiritual exercises, such as to go up to the temple on appointed days, to withdraw at times into solitude, to give themselves to prayer, and so forth. Hence, it is reasonable that this little Congregation should also have its spiritual exercises, which it shall perform most diligently and which it shall prefer, unless necessity or obedience disposes otherwise, to every other occupation, since these exercises lead more effectively to the genuine observance of other rules and constitutions, and to the attainment of our perfection.*[1]

St. Vincent asks you to make the incarnation and the Trinity the center of your life. Remember that he continually proposed Jesus, the Word made flesh, as the exemplar for all that the members of his Company were to do. He asks you to come to know God our Father in prayer and to call upon God's spirit to fill the Company, so that the life of the Risen Lord might be conspicuous among us.

St. Vincent sets out concrete means to which, in adapted form, our new Constitutions ask you to commit yourself:

1. take part in the eucharist daily;
2. join your brothers each morning and evening in praising God in common;
3. in imitation of Jesus who spent even whole nights in prayer, support your brothers by giving an hour daily to personal prayer; seek to spend some of that time in the presence of the Blessed Sacrament;
4. receive the sacrament of penance frequently, as the Church in each age shall recommend;
5. read a portion of the New Testament daily, and in addition spend some time reading from a book that pertains to spiritual matters;
6. have some daily devotion to Mary, the Mother of Jesus, such as the rosary; in particular, imitate her attentiveness in listening to the word of God, her humility, her gratitude, her purity; whenever occasion offers, encourage others to know her and love her.
7. make it your practice to examine your conscience daily in order that you might grow in Christ's life;
8. engage in spiritual direction regularly throughout your life;
9. each year join your brothers in an annual retreat.

In committing yourself to St. Vincent's Company, my brother, know that

---

1. CR X, 1.

he asks you to commit yourself to means like these. If you enter into them wholeheartedly and give yourself generously to them, you will certainly grow.

CHAPTER IX - SIMPLICITY

This is the virtue St. Vincent loved most.[1] "It is my gospel," he says.[2] Listen, my brother, to how St. Vincent describes simplicity:

Jesus, the Lord, expects us to have the simplicity of a dove. This means giving a straightforward opinion about things in the way we honestly see them, without needless reservations. It also means doing things without any double-dealing or manipulation, our intention being focused solely on God. Each of us, then, should take care to behave always in this spirit of simplicity, remembering that God likes to deal with the simple, and that he conceals the secrets of heaven from the wise and prudent of this world and reveals them to little ones.

But while Christ recommends the simplicity of a dove he tells us to have the prudence of a serpent as well. What he means is that we should speak and behave with discretion. We ought, therefore, to keep quiet about matters which should not be made know, especially if they are unsuitable or unlawful . . . In actual practice this virtue is about choosing the right way to do things. We should make it a sacred principle, then, admitting of no exceptions, that since we are working for God we will always choose God-related ways for carrying out our work, and see and judge things from Christ's point of view and not from a worldly-wise one; and not according to the feeble reasoning of our own mind either. That is how we can be prudent as serpents and simple as doves.[3]

St. Vincent proposed simplicity to his sons as their first characteristic. He loved to speak on the subject:

God is simple. Wherever you discover Christian simplicity, walk with confidence, whereas they that use craftiness and duplicity are in constant fear lest their cunning be detected, and lest in consequence other people cease to have confidence in them.

For my part—as I can affirm—long experience has demonstrated to my satisfaction, that a strong and practical faith, and a true spirit of religion, are more commonly found among poor and simple people. God is pleased to enrich them with fervent faith. They believe and relish the words of everlasting life that Christ has left us in his gospel. As a general rule, they bear illness patiently,

---

1. SV I, 284.
2. SV IX, 606.
3. CR II, 4-5.

privations, too, and other afflictions. Such things they endure without murmuring or complaining, except a little and rarely.

Moreover, everyone feels an attraction for persons who are simple and candid, persons who refuse to employ cunning or deceit. They are popular because they act ingenuously, and speak sincerely; their lips are ever in accord with their hearts. They are esteemed and loved everywhere . . . . [1]

In St. Vincent's spirit then, my brother, speak truthfully, even at times when the truth may be inconvenient or embarrassing to you. That is not an easy discipline. Seek to do only what God wants. Strive to have less and less preoccupation with yourself. Do not be anxious for the esteem of others. God communicates with the simple. He reveals himself to the little.

---

1. These themes recur frequently when St. Vincent speaks of simplicity. Cf. SV XI, 50; XII, 171.

CHAPTER X - HUMILITY

Take St. Vincent's words very much to heart, my brother:

Each one shall also show great diligence in learning this lesson taught by Christ. "Learn of me, for I am meek and humble of heart." By it we are reminded, as he himself affirms, that the earth is possessed through meekness, because by the exercise of this virtue men's hearts are well disposed to be turned back to the Lord, something which is not accomplished by those who deal harshly and roughly with the neighbor. Moreover, heaven is acquired by humility, for the love of self-abasement is wont to raise us up, leading us step by step from virtue to virtue, until we arrive at our goal.[1]

Humility is basic to gospel spirituality. The kingdom of God belongs to the poor in spirit. God resists the proud; he raises up the humble. St. Vincent knew these things well. In fact, he was convinced that humility is "the foundation of evangelical perfection and the core of the spiritual life."[2] Consequently, there is no virtue that he spoke of more eloquently. Sense in his words, my brother, the great conviction with which he spoke on the subject:

How does it happen then that so few try to practice it and still fewer possess it? It is because it is ravishing to speculate on, but its practice is disagreeable to nature; its very appearance is disagreeable to nature. To practice it means that we should always choose the lowest place, put ourselves below others, even the least, bear with calumnies, seek after contempt, love abjection; and to all these things we are naturally adverse. Yet it is essential for us to overcome this repugnance; it is essential for each of us to make strong efforts to arrive at the actual exercise of this virtue. Otherwise, we shall never acquire it.[3]

Stand before God humbly in your daily prayer, my brother. Have the attitude of a servant. Let there be no task too menial for you to take on cheerfully. Stand before God and your brothers with a grateful heart, as one who has received many gifts. He who is mighty has done great things. Never tire of responding by daily common-place labor.

St. Vincent also asks us to be humble corporately. He urges us to see ourselves as a little Company, existing by God's love and kindness—able to

---

1. CR II, 6.
2. CR II, 7.
3. SV XI, 54.

do nothing on your own, but able to do all things by God's power. It is with great urgency that he writes:

> *Understand this well, gentlemen and my brothers: we shall never be fit to do the work of God if we have not profound humility and self-contempt. No, if the Company of the Mission is not humble, if it has not the belief and conviction that it can do no good, that it is more apt to spoil everything than otherwise, it will never accomplish anything great; but where it possesses and lives in the spirit of which I have just spoken, then, rest assured, gentlemen, it will be fit to do the work of God, because God makes use of such subjects for his great works.*[1]

---

1. St. Vincent emphasizes the need for corporate humility again and again. Cf. SV IX, 57; IX, 303; X, 200; XI, 60; XI, 114-115; XI, 434; XII, 438.

CHAPTER XI - MEEKNESS

My brother, St. Vincent tells us that he was choleric by temperament. Confronted with the gospel call to be meek and humble of heart, he asked God to change his heart:

I turned to God and earnestly begged him to change this irritable and forbidding disposition of mine, and to grant me a kindly and benign spirit. And with the grace of our Lord, by giving a little attention to suppressing the impetuous impulses of my nature, I have been partially cured of my gloomy disposition.[1]

God worked healing in this holy man, my brother. His contemporaries tell us that he was affable and easy to approach. He was mild even when administering correction. By his compassion and the kindness of his words, even when reprimanding, he often won the hearts of the stubborn.

St. Vincent warned the members of his Company not to think that those who are meek are weak:

There are no persons more constant nor firm in well-doing than those who are meek and gracious. While on the contrary those who allow themselves to yield to anger and the passions of the irascible appetite are mostly inconstant, because they only act by fits and starts. They are like torrents, which are strong and impetuous only when in full flood but which dry up immediately afterwards, while rivers, which represent the gentle and gracious, flow on noiselessly, tranquilly and unfailingly.[2]

Learn, my brother, to be meek. Anger can be a force for good or for evil in your life. To control it and find creative ways of expressing it is a great challenge.

When directed against injustice, as Jesus' example shows us, anger strengthens a person to struggle courageously, to confront the Pharisee, to "cast out the money-changers from God's house." But, as our own experience teaches us, anger can also be destructive. It can drive us to lash out at the weak or the innocent.

Learn to understand your anger and to harness it for good, for truth, for justice. You may fail many times in your attempts, but know that the power of God is much greater than the weakness that you experience. Jesus says that the meek shall be happy. St. Vincent believed this word of the Lord and won the hearts of the poor because his meekness developed as warmth, approachability, openness, deep respect for the person of others. His contem-

---

1. Abelly, bk. III, 177-178.
2. SV XI, 65.

poraries found him gentle and welcoming. But he also knew, as he sometimes expressed it to St. Louise de Marillac, "how to mix the bitter with the sweet."[1] Seek, my brother, to develop this remarkable combination of gentleness and firmness.[2]

1. SV I, 393-94.
2. SV VII, 226.

CHAPTER XII - MORTIFICATION

My brother, Jesus calls you to follow him even unto death. He asks you to die to sin daily. St. Vincent knew these gospel imperatives very well. Listen to his words:

> Since Christ has said: "If anyone wishes to come after me, let him deny himself, and take up his cross daily"; and since St. Paul in the same spirit has added: "If you live according to the flesh you will die, but if by the spirit you put to death the deeds of the flesh, you will live," everyone shall devote himself to a continual denial of his own will and judgement, also the mortification of all his senses.[1]

Take on no exaggerated mortifications, my brother, but still let mortification be a real part of your daily life. It is an indispensable means for reaching the goals you seek. It will set you free, even to die for Christ.

St. Vincent offers you many means, which can be adapted to present-day circumstances:

1. be faithful to the duties of your state in life; prefer them when they conflict with other more pleasurable things;
2. work hard as servants do;
3. be sparing in your obtaining or accepting material possessions, like clothing or money, or items for your room;
4. rise promptly in the morning that you might praise God and strengthen your brothers by joining them in prayer;
5. be slow to ask for privileges, or to be the exception from what is the norm in the Company;
6. withhold critical or divisive words;
7. seek equally to be with those who are less pleasing to you as with those to whom you are attracted;
8. be disciplined in eating and drinking, and avoid all anxiety or complaint about what you shall eat or what you shall drink;
9. employ moderation and a critical sense in using television, radio, movies, and other media.

---

1. CR II, 8.

CHAPTER XIII - ZEAL

"If love of God is a fire," St. Vincent tells us, "then zeal is its flame."[1]

He loved, my brother, with a burning love. From the bottom of his heart he cried out to the members of his Company:

> Behold the beautiful field which God is opening up to us in Madagascar, the Hebrides and elsewhere! Let us beg him to enkindle in our hearts a desire to serve him. Let us give ourselves to him to do whatever he pleases with us. St. Vincent Ferrer encouraged himself by the thought that one day priests would come who by the fervor of their zeal, would set the whole world on fire. If we do not deserve that God should give us the grace to be those priests, let us at least beg him to make us their exemplars and forerunners. But, however that may be, let us hold it as certain that we shall not be true Christians until we are ready to lose all and to give even our life for the love and glory of Jesus Christ, resolving, with the holy Apostle, to desire tortures and even death itself rather than be separated from the charity of the divine Savior.[2]

St. Vincent labored doggedly even to the end. Listen to his simple statement as an old man:

> As for myself, my age notwithstanding, I do not consider that I am excused from the obligation of laboring in the service of the poor; what is there to prevent me from so doing? If I am unable to preach every day, I will preach twice a week; and if I lack sufficient strength to make myself heard in large churches, I will speak in small ones; and if even that should prove impracticable, what will hinder me from gathering those good people around me, and speaking to them simply and familiarly just as I am now talking to you![3]

The ways of serving are many, my brother. Take St. Vincent's words to heart. When you are a young man, use the resources of youth, its vigor and enthusiasm, in the service of the poor. When you have grown old, bring the resources of age, experience and understanding, to bear on your labors. Labor long as a servant of the poor. In all things be faithful, even to the end.

But there is a subtle enemy, St. Vincent warns us, that lurks at the far edge of zeal. He called it "indiscreet zeal."[4] Today we might describe it as

---

1. SV XII, 307-308.
2. SV XI, 75.
3. SV XI, 136.
4. CR XII, 11.

over-working. It often leads to discouragement, anger with those who work less, resentment, and finally apathy. It can be a deadly enemy.

So know your limitations. Live a balanced life, so that you might have the energy that nourishes zeal. While the Lord asks you to cooperate in his work, it still remains *his* work. When the time comes to rest, place the work in his hands. "The Lord gives to his beloved in sleep" (Ps 127:2).

CHAPTER XIV - TRUST IN PROVIDENCE

Listen, my brother, to these striking words of St. Vincent:

If divine providence ever allows a house or member of the Congregation, or the Congregation itself, to be subjected to, and tested by, slander or persecution, we are to be extra careful to avoid any retaliation, verbal abuse, or complaint against the persecutors or slanderers. We should even praise and bless God, and joyfully thank him for it as an opportunity for great good, coming down from the Father of lights. We should even pray sincerely to him for those who harm us and, if the opportunity and possibility present themselves, should willingly help them, remembering that Christ commanded us, and all the faithful to do this: "Love your enemies, do good to those who hate you, and pray for persecutors and slanderers." And to get us to do this more willingly and more easily he said that we would be blessed in doing so and that we should be joyful and glad about it since our reward is great in heaven. And, more importantly, he was gracious enough to be the first to act in this way towards others so as to be a model for us. Afterwards the apostles, disciples, and numberless Christians followed his example.[1]

Christ said: "Seek first the kingdom of God and his justice, and all those things which you need will be given to you as well." That is the basis for each of us having the following set of priorities: matters involving our relationship with God are more important than temporal affairs; spiritual health is more important than physical; God's glory is more important than human approval. Each one should, moreover, be determined to prefer, like St. Paul to do without necessities, to be slandered or tortured, or even killed, rather than lose Christ's love. In practice, then, we should not worry too much about temporal affairs. We ought to have confidence in God that he will look after us since we know for certain that as long as we are grounded in that sort of love and trust we will be always under the protection of God in heaven, we will remain unaffected by evil and never lack what we need even when everything we possess seems headed for disaster.[2]

Vincent knew great peace. He trusted in God as his own Father, who watched over and cared for him. He believed deeply that God was the author of the Confraternities of Charity, the Congregation of the Mission, the

---

1. CR II, 13.
2. CR II, 2.

Daughters of Charity and all the good that he had done in the service of the poor. He was confident that his Father, who had begun these good works would bring them to completion. He had utter trust in God's unseen plans, which work through human history to reveal his love. On the one hand, he urged his followers to be patient in discerning and following God's designs. He knew that grace has its moments and he praised those who had learned the rhythm of God's movements.[1] But on the other hand, he knew that this same loving, provident Father acts in and through human instruments, as he had in Jesus his Son. So he also praised those who had learned to foresee and prepare the way for the works of providence.[2]

Learn from this holy man, my brother, to place yourself in God's hands daily. Your life will know many joys and many sorrows. Accept them as gifts or as challenges from the hand of God. Seek little for yourself. Do not be anxious about what you shall eat or what you shall drink or what you shall put on. Seek first the kingdom of God. Then all other things will be given you besides.

---

1. SV II, 453.
2. SV VII, 310.

My brother, learn from St. Vincent. He knew Jesus well. He loved him deeply as the Evangelizer of the Poor. He penetrated the meaning of the good news and burned with an intense desire to share it with the poor. He lived simply. Yet he did great things.

The wisdom of the world will often hold out power or fame or comfort as more sensible than St. Vincent's style of life. It will suggest to you that other means are more effective than chastity, poverty, obedience and service of the poor. But you have not chosen to follow the wisdom of the world, my brother. You have chosen to live the gospels. Learn from this holy man the ways in which his Company should embody them.

If you become conscious that you are growing in St. Vincent's way, rejoice in the gift God is giving you. Pray too that God might strengthen all of us, your brothers, in the same way. But always, as a humble man, recall what St. Vincent told his Company:

> . . . *we must get it firmly into our heads*
> *that when we have carried out all we have been asked to do, we should,*
> *following Christ's advice, say to ourselves that we are useless servants,*
> *that we have done what we were supposed to do,*
> *and that, in fact,*
> *we could not have done anything without him.*[1]

---

1. CR XII, 14.

We are weak, O God,
and capable of giving in at the first assault.

By your pure loving kindness
you have called us;
may your infinite goodness, please,
now help us persevere.

For our part, with your holy grace,
we will try with all our strength
to summon up
all the service and all the faithfulness that you ask of us.
So give us, O God, give us the grace to persevere until death.

This is what I ask of you
through the merits of Our Lord Jesus Christ
with confidence that you will remember me.

SV IX, 360